Can Anyone be a Leader?

CAN ANYONE
BE A LEADER?

Comments, Stories and Quotes
to help develop leaders

David Pytches

eagle
Eagle Publishing, Trowbridge

Published by Eagle Publishing Ltd, 6 Kestrel House, Millll Street, Trowbridge, BA14 8BE.

British Library Cataloguing in Publication Data. A catalogue record for this book is available from the British Library.

Scripture quotations unless otherwise noted are from The Holy Bible, New International Version, Copyright © 1973, 1978, 1984 by International Bible Society. Used by permission of Hodder & Stoughton, a Division of Hodder Headline.

Typeset by Eagle Publishing Ltd
Printed by Bookmarque
ISBN No: 0 86347 613 9

DEDICATION

To the current leaders of New Wine and Soul Survivor
whose tireless labours for encouraging and
building up the Church of Jesus Christ
across the world both inspires and amazes.
May God continue to bless you all.

Contents

Introduction

For the church that will still be growing ten years from now, leadership deveoplment is the core issue.

(JOHN WIMBER)

The single most important factor preventing growth in the church today is the inability to identify, recruit, train, deploy, monitor and nurture leaders and workers.

(JOHN WIMBER)

There are three types of people: those who make things happen, those who watch things happen, and those who haven't a clue what's happening.

(ANON)

Church leadership … is so important … because it has the power to change the world.

(BILL HYBELS, COURAGEOUS LEADERSHIP)

Leadership is a fascinating subject, not least because leaders are such fascinating people.

(JOHN RICHARDSON, NEW DIRECTIONS OCTOBER 2003)

The ministry of the laity as the true Christian priesthood is quite overshadowed by the small minority who compose the clergy, who have had spent on them an overwhelming proportion of the funds raised to train and to maintain the church's ministry.[1]

(J. TILLER AND M. BIRCHALL)

Be more concerned with your character than with your reputation. Your character is that what you really are while your reputation is merely what others think you are.

(JOHN WOODEN, BASKETBALL COACH)

READY MIX FOR DEVELOPING LEADERS

Some pundits resist identifying any essential qualities in leaders, believing that too many exceptions mean that there is, in fact, no such thing as a 'leadership personality', a 'leadership style' or 'a leadership trait'. But too many exceptions only prove the rule.

Christian Schwarz asserts that effective growth is based on a quality index for the church.[2] If churches need certain qualities to grow, then leaders will need certain qualities to lead. If the greatest crisis in the world today is a crisis of leadership, the greatest crisis in leadership is a crisis of character. Wherever churches have broken down it has usually been traceable to a lack in one or more of the basic qualities for leadership highlighted in this book. Each chapter deals with one of these characteristics and is prefaced with appropriate comments and observations, followed by pithy one–liners, handy illustrations and a few funny situations. In this way it provides a simple checklist with relevant material from which local church leaders can 'pick-n-mix' according to their priorities for a local training programme.

QUALITIES NEEDED IN LEADERS

Every now and again a journal will put out a survey of senior professions concerning the particular qualities expected in their leaders and not surprisingly character is regularly shown to be the priority. Bill Hybels says his selection process is based on 'three C's': first Character, then Competence, and finally Chemistry (this latter concerns how well the candidate might relate to him, the rest of his team and the people). Whenever he is searching for someone to fill a leadership gap, he says, 'I remind myself, Character first'. Other traits are usually subordinate aspects of character.

In church life, where the highest goal is the making of godly disciples, character has to be significant.

> We are concerned to help people develop (not only) a Christian mind, but also a Christian heart, a Christian spirit, a Christian conscience and a Christian will, in fact to become whole Christian persons, thoroughly integrated under the Lordship of Christ.
>
> (JOHN STOTT)

CHANGING LEADERSHIP PRACTICE

Our index at the end reveals how many people today are writing seriously on leadership. But this book is different, as the reader will soon notice. The radical shape of tomorrow's church calls for new kinds of leadership training emerging into more flexible structures for spontaneous church growth. This was recognised at least 30 years ago by Bishop David Sheppard who said,

> The organised church must encourage spur of the moment 'happenings'. It must risk giving the erratic leaders their head. This will mean that the church leadership is not able to keep control of events. Things get out of hand. But they may allow the Holy Spirit to intervene.[3]

In the ranks of these new leaders involved in new ways of doing church will be men and women from surprising cultural and educational backgrounds. God is choosing leaders for the future who may well not be the kind of people the church has been accustomed to regard as potential leadership material. Nor will so many in the future be trained in the traditional ways we have seen within our theological colleges.[4]

Much as we have valued them, and also our Bible Institutes, it is doubtful if enough money could be found to keep many of them going for much longer. Of course the church will always need the insights of specialists well-read in theology and teachers well-trained to expound Scripture, but most of our future leaders will emerge from much less expensive programmes, and with much more hands-on involvement.

MAKING EFFECTIVE LEADERS

Philip King discusses what the preparation of leaders should be termed – 'teaching' sounds too academic and 'training' too activist. He prefers the word 'development' which has the advantage in that 'it can include spiritual, intellectual and practical aspects, as well as learning to create good relationships, and suggests a continuing process'.[5]

Ministers in God's kingdom have to learn to lead their congregations in godliness, make new disciples, prepare an emerging generation for leadership and develop them.

Thankfully there are a number of church leaders in the UK who are already grooming men and women with character, vision and ability to lead in the planting of new churches. And what we have in the UK is only a small reflection of what is happening across the world. Such new leadership models cover not only the local church but extend into countless other arenas. It was significant that in the small groups where many of John Wesley's disciples became class leaders, a fair number went on to become some of the foremost trade union leaders of their day.[6]

GOD'S IRREGULARS

Not everyone becomes a leader in the same way. Some enter by an irregular route. One such was Jim Cymbala, newly married and recently settled in a Brooklyn apartment. Out of the blue his father-in-law, who had seen his potential, phoned him to suggest that maybe God wanted him in full-time Christian service. 'There's a church in Newark that needs a pastor,' he said. 'They are precious people. Why don't you think about quitting your job and stepping out in faith to see what God will do?'

'I'm not qualified – me – a minister? I have no idea how to be a pastor,' protested Jim.

His father-in-law, the overseer of a few small independent churches, replied, 'When God calls someone, that's all that really matters. Don't let yourself be afraid.'

Jim Cymbala stepped out in faith. He was humble and teachable – open to learning on the job. Eventually his congregation became one of the most significant churches in New York.

INDEBTED TO SO MANY

This book is not the gripping account of a 'successful' church but the distillation of wisdom from many successful leaders. A number of these sources – where they have been traceable – have come from books listed in the index. But over the years one gathers choice phrases and illustrations at conferences and workshops, gems dropped from numerous speakers or found among authors whose names are long since forgotten. Some of this material has surfaced anonymously from a distant past. I include it with apologies to their unattributable originators.

Finally, John Piper ends his book *A Godward Life*, with the prayer that 'God may be pleased to take ... a sentence or paragraph ... (and) set on fire your mind'. That's my prayer also – maybe something in this book will inspire the new leadership for tomorrow's church.

David Pytches

CHAPTER 1

What are leaders?

Are leaders born or made?
Can anyone be a leader or are they only the favoured few?
Is there a particular trick to it or a particular style -
something that if we could learn, would transform our role in life?
(CHARLES HANDY)

True leaders have a unique talent for gathering around themselves
others who thereby find new inspiration, frequently achieving things
that would otherwise have seemed elusive or impossible.
(JOHN RICHARDSON)

Being in leadership is not the same thing as merely being in charge. Military historians can cite sad examples of generals who have been 'in charge' but failed to lead. Tragically the same have been said of church ministers too.

COMMENT

Leaders lead. 'For every man who has the ability to lead there are a thousand waiting to be led' (Roy. L. Smith). Leaders are not meant to be bosses. Bosses drive while leaders lead. The boss depends upon authority whereas the leader depends upon good will. The boss evokes fear; the leader inspires faith. The boss fixes the blame for the breakdown; the leader fixes the breakdown.

We drive cattle but we lead people. A leader, like a shepherd, goes ahead of his flock. They lead their sheep into green pastures to feed them, beside still waters to refresh them, and into paths of righteousness to train them in godliness (Psalm 23). The sheep follow their shepherds and their shepherds follow Christ (Luke 5:11; John 21:22).

Some pastors have limited leadership qualities. Some are even led by their sheep! A few years ago I read a letter in the press from a bishop who seemed to be seriously boasting that the trick was to find out which way the flock was going and then to take up a position ahead of them. Not all pastors are good church leaders. Nevertheless all good church leaders must be pastors at heart. While seeking to follow Christ themselves they ensure that their sheep have proper care, even if they can no longer provide it all themselves. True leaders are watching to see that every thing possible is done for their sheep. That is clearly God's purpose. Jesus pastored, and trained others to do the same, and his reward was the knowledge that he was doing the will of his Father. For that reason he even lay down his life for his sheep (John 10:11,15b,17,18). Christ, then, is our model leader.

THE MODEL LEADER

Christ was an apostle and was called an apostle (Hebrews 3:1) but he never particularly referred to himself as an apostle.

He was a prophet and they talked of him as one (John 4:19; 7:40) but he did not call himself a prophet.

He was a teacher. They called him rabbi. He did not use the title of himself but he accepted that he was their teacher when they addressed him as such (John 13:13).

He was an evangelist, preaching the kingdom of God, and bringing people to repentance and faith, but he never called himself an evangelist.

However he did specifically refer to himself as a pastor. He said he was 'the good shepherd' (John 10:11). And Peter referred to him as the Chief Shepherd (1 Peter 5:2-4) while the writer to the Hebrews called him the great Shepherd (Hebrews 13:20). So it is clear that his model for us is one of a pastor. His 'shepherd' heart undergirded all the other roles he exercised. And other callings we have in the church – apostles, prophets, evangelists and teachers – are much less effective if divorced from a pastoral heart.

WHAT IS LEADERSHIP?

Leadership is about leading people somewhere.

> Reaching a fork in the road Alice in Wonderland wanted to know which way to go.
> 'Which road should I take?' she asked the Cheshire Cat.

'Where are you going?' the cat replied.

'I don't know,' she answered.

'Then it doesn't matter which road you take,' said the cat.

If leaders don't know where they are going they simply mislead. But Jesus knew where he was going and he wanted to take his followers there (John 14:6).

Leadership, according to Christ's example, is the ability to ensure that the flock is properly cared for and to humbly induce the followers to achieve goals that represent the values and the motivations, the wants and needs, the aspirations and expectations of the leader himself. So we are to exemplify, teach and enable followers to focus on the goals, practices and values of the kingdom of God.

And the genius of leadership is the manner in which these ends are accomplished in their own localities, by leaders with their own characters, their own giftings, their own inadequacies, and their own idiosyncrasies.

LEADERSHIP IN THE LIFE OF THE CHURCH

Good leadership is the key to success in any institution. Bill Hybels has commented, 'What flourishing churches have in common is that they are led by people who possess and deploy the spiritual gift of leadership.' A respected headmaster spoke of the responsibility for choosing the right kind of leader in a school:

'It is a scary fact that the ethos of a school depends so much on the head. Scary for governors responsible for the appointment, scary for the staff, parents and pupils, that one person may change the lives of so many, and scary for the head to have such a burden. A good appointment may turn an institution around very quickly; so may a bad one.'

Obviously there can be no substitute for the call of God. He alone decides who should do what in his church. '[Christ] gave some to be apostles, some to be prophets, some to be evangelists, and some to be pastors and teachers, to prepare God's people for works of service, so that the body of Christ may be built up until we all reach unity in the faith and the knowledge of the Son of God and become mature, attaining to the whole measure of the fulness of Christ' (Ephesians

4:11–13 NIV). And once a call to leadership is accepted it is usually recognised in a public commissioning by the church (cf Acts 13:2,3).

'Leader' is a New Testament term for pastor

Jesus said to them, 'In this world the kings and great men order their people around, and yet they are called "friends of the people". But among you, those who are the greatest should take the lowest rank, and the leader should be like a servant. Normally the master sits at the table and is served by his servants. But not here! For I am your servant.'

(Luke 22:25–27 NLT).

'If his gift is leadership let him govern diligently.'

(Romans 12:8 NIV).

'I did this privately, to those who seemed to be leaders, for fear that I was running or had run my race in vain.'

(Galatians 2:2b NIV).

'Remember the leaders who spoke the word of God to you. Consider the outcome of their way of life and imitate their faith..'

(Hebrews 13:7 TNIV).

'Have confidence in your leaders and submit to their authority, because they keep watch over you as those who must give an account..'

(Hebrews 13:17 TNIV).

'Give my warm greetings to all your leaders and all God's people..'

(Hebrews 13:24 Translators NT).

'If the blind lead the blind both shall fall into the ditch.'

(Jesus – Matthew 15:14 KJV).

While the church is led by leaders, they are not usually referred to as such, even though the responsibilities of leadership are implied by their office.

CHOOSING NEW LEADERS

Sooner or later future leaders need to be trained. Where does one start? Whom does one choose? How does one recognise leadership ability in those who have never led? Of course the first resource for the Christian leader faced with such choices is prayer. Jesus spent a whole night in prayer before he chose the twelve apostles. Sometimes the Lord makes it fairly obvious that a person has leadership potential. The Lord appears to have seen that in Peter (Matthew 16:18). Time will show whether one's followers have, or are likely to develop, the necessary qualities. Tacitus once wrote of the Emperor Galba that he was *'capax imperii nisi imperasset'* – even had he never been made emperor no one would have doubted his ability to lead.

Any appointment is, to some extent, a holy gamble (interestingly Judas' replacement was chosen by lot! (Acts 1:26), a practice still continued in some Mennonite churches today). But then every step in life has an element of uncertainty about it – we never know what tomorrow may bring. There seems no uniformity in the way a person is called, or humanly selected. Sometimes the Lord reveals who will be the new leaders to other people, apart from the leader himself. This may come through dreams, prophecy or revelation. Samuel came to the house of Jesse and anointed David, the youngest son, to be the next king – the last person his father or older brothers would have imagined!

Some, like Moses, Peter or Paul, have personally heard God's call in an unforgettable encounter. Some have found themselves placed in authority by secular humans like Joseph, while others have been commissioned by the church like Barnabas, Timothy or Titus. But all of them had to have their call recognised. They have to come into leadership somehow – they have to start somewhere.

Mike Brearley has said, 'For everyone who has once captained a [cricket] side for the first time, someone must have made a favourable judgement about his potential. Someone picked that person out!'[6]

QUOTES – LEADERS
  • Leaders have to lead. (Simon Peres, interview with David Frost BBC TV, 15 October 2000)
  • Someone in an organisation has to be the leader.

'Partnerships sound great and utopian but unless there is a clear delineation of responsibility they will not work.' (Sven-Goran Eriksson)

- Winners in life think constantly of I can, I will, and I am. (Dennis Waitley)
- Anyone can hold the helm when the sea is calm! (Admiral Lord Nelson)
- There are two kinds of people in the world: those who stand up and face the music and those who run for cover. (Frank Slade)
- He who thinks he leads and has no followers is only taking a walk. (John C. Maxwell)
- The new leader is one who commits people to action, who converts followers into leaders, and who inspires leaders to be agents of change. (Wallis Bennis)
- He led but he did not drive. (G. Vibert Douglas)
- A leader's potential is measured by those working with him. (John Maxwell)
- A leader is the organisation's main source of positive energy. (Noel M. Tichy)
- Leaders must always be aware of the power they wield. (Daniel Goldin)
- Leaders of the future will not be able to assume that leadership means hierarchy and control of others. (Edgar H. Schein)
- The leaders of the future will be people who can both lead and follow, be central and marginal … Be individualistic and team players and above all be perpetual learners. (Edgar H. Schein)
- Those who govern best are those who govern least. (North American Constitutionalist)
- If it's going to be – it's up to me. (Robert Schuller)
- The leader's most important attribute is motivating others. (Ole Iverson)
- Unfortunately there's no book that tells you how to be mayor. (Rudolph Giuliani, ex-mayor of New York City)
- A leader should be anticipating all the time. (Rudolph Giuliani)
- The chief characteristic of leaders, Jesus insisted, is humility

not authority, and gentleness not power. (John Stott)
- It takes a leader to raise up a leader. (John Maxwell)
- A good leader takes a little more than his share of the blame; and little less than his share of the credit. (Arnold H. Glasgow)
- If the bugle gives an indistinct sound who will get ready for battle? (1 Corinthians 14:8 RSV)
- He is no leader who nails his colours to the fence! (With apologies to the late Garth Bennett)
- A leader is a dealer in hope. (Napoleon Bonaparte)
- There is no room for copying anyone else's play at Test Level (cricket). (Kapil Dev)
- Captaincy is ninety per cent luck and ten per cent skill. But don't try it without the ten per cent. (Richie Bernaud, Australian cricketer and commentator)

QUOTES – LEADERSHIP
- The true measure of leadership is influence. (John C. Maxwell)
- Leadership is not about positions to be occupied but influence to be exercised. (Ken Gott)
- Leadership is the capacity to translate vision into reality. (Warren G. Bennis)
- Leadership is taking people from where they are to where they should be. (Anon)
- Leadership is getting people to work for you when they are not obliged to do so. (Fred Smith, *Learning to Lead*, Word, 1986)
- Leadership is one of the things you cannot delegate. You either exercise it or abdicate (from) it.[9] (Robert Goizueta)
- Leadership develops daily, not in a day. (John Maxwell)
- Leadership is a fine thing, but it has its price. And part of the price is loneliness. (Anon)
- No man ruleth safely but he that is willingly ruled. (Thomas à Kempis)
- Leadership requires vision and perseverance. 'Veni, Vidi, Velcro – I came, I saw, I stuck!' (Bishop Sentamu of Birmingham)
- Leadership is responsibility. (Anon)

- Most of us are second-rate, so it is not necessarily any great insult to point out that politics is largely practised by second-raters. (Jeremy Paxman, *The Political Animal*)
- A big part of leadership is consistency. (Rudolph Giuliani)
- Leadership is a relationship founded on trust and confidence. (Kouzes & Posner)
- Our major problem in the world today is that nobody wants to take responsibility for anything – but don't quote me. (Anon)
- The BBC simply does not want to take a lead anymore: to do so would suggest it was in possession of authority – and we are anti-authoritarian now aren't we? (Janet Daley, *Daily Telegraph* 28 January 1977)
- You'll have the most miserable time of your life. (Brian Close to Ian Botham about accepting the England cricket captaincy in 1980)

ILLUSTRATIONS
Leadership: Serious Business
J. John expressed his shock when he came across a poem called 'The Leader':

I wanna be a leader,
I wanna be a leader,
Can I be a leader?
Can I? I can?
Promise? Promise?
Yippie, I'm a leader.
I'm a leader.
OK, what shall I do?' (William Dunbar)

Leaders are seekers after God's will.
'Like anybody I would like to live a long life. But I'm not concerned about that now. I just want God's will. And he has allowed me to go up to the mountain and I have seen the Promised Land. I may not get there with you, but I want you to know tonight, that we as a people will get to the Promised Land!' (Martin Luther King on the eve of his assassination)

Born to lead
If anyone was destined from birth to take creative control of the Old Vic, Kevin Spacey believes he is the man. 'For me, this is a remarkable thing. I feel that everything in my life has been leading up to this,' he says quietly. 'This is what I was meant to do.' (John Hiscock)

Failed to achieve
In his diary for 1st January 1963, the 14-year-old Gyles Brandreth wrote out the vision of his destiny in leadership: 'I am going to be Prime Minister and before that, I shall be a great reforming Home Secretary, like Winston Churchill.' Somehow along the way Brandreth's vision was abandoned. He kept his seat in Parliament for only a brief time. Today he writes and entertains engagingly. (Review, Sunday Telegraph 29 December 2002)

Resolutely ordinary
Simon Fuller, the 41-year-old Englishman in the entertainment world, who was behind the Spice Girls, Pop Idol and American Idol successes, now worth £200 million, has been described as 'successful because, unlike lesser operators in the industry, he's resolutely ordinary. He understands popular tastes better than anyone. But he has the vision and the gambling instincts to see his dreams through.'

Mr Average
Sir Ernest Shackleton, the Antarctic explorer, was 'a very average person; he taught himself how to be an exceptional one. He rose above his peers and earned the unfailing loyalty of his men. His story is, in essence, an inspirational tale about unleashing strengths in individuals that they never knew they had in order to achieve goals – from the small to the miraculous.' (M. Morrell and S. Capparell)

Soft management
'I am a soft manager. Unlike the classic leaders of business legend with their towering self-confidence, their unflinching tenacity, their hard, lonely lives at the top, I try to be vulnerable to criticism. I do my best to be tentative and I cherish my own fair share of human frailty. But like them, I too have worked hard to master my management style, and on the whole I think it [mine] compares favourably with theirs.' (William H. Peace)

Right mindset
At the conclusion of a management seminar a young man told me, 'I don't think these principles will work in my department.'

'You're right,' I said. 'They probably won't.'

He gave me a puzzled look. 'But you just told us they would work in any organisation. Now you are contradicting yourself,' he said beginning to look rather annoyed.

So I responded: 'No I am not contradicting myself. They probably won't work for you because you don't think they will work. Therefore you probably won't make the commitment needed for them to work.' (Myron Rush)

Sure way to fail
One of the best case studies concerning the effect an attitude can have on the actions of others is on record in the Old Testament book of Numbers. Moses had sent out twelve spies to determine how the land lay, the size and strength of the cities, and the type of crops being grown there (Numbers 13:17–20 NIV). Their mission was not to determine whether or not they should conquer the land. Their mission was to discover what conditions would prevail when they eventually invaded the land. The spies spent forty days there and returned with glowing reports concerning its fertility and abundant produce: 'We went into the land to which you sent us, and it does flow with milk and honey!' (v 27)

'But the people who live there are powerful, and the cities are fortified and very large. We even saw descendants of Anak there' (v 28). Ten of the spies voted against any attack: 'We can't attack these people' (v 31). And explained why to Moses: '… they are stronger than we are … We seemed like grasshoppers in our own eyes, and we looked the same to them' (vv 31,32).

Negative opinions produce negative consequences. They thought of themselves as grasshoppers beside the enemy. Their negative assumptions were the fruit of their negative attitudes.

Some good leaders are amateurs
Amateur leaders will often risk running foul of the organised hierarchy. 'All creative companies need people who are not clones of their predecessors.' The maddening thing about so many good leaders seems to be that they are annoying misfits who will not or

cannot appreciate corporate traditions or accepted procedures.

Leadership is both learned and earned. It is learned from earlier experiences in the smaller scales of life and it is earned by the growing respect and trust conceded by their followers.

Leaders' non-conformity to popular images

The gangly, unkempt Abraham Lincoln gave the physical impression of being a social misfit but developed skills on a national level which made him a memorable leader. Smith Wigglesworth, the one-time plumber and pioneer of the Pentecostal movement, could be menacing but miraculously effective, even though he had 'an abrupt, unpolished manner and was an illiterate, inarticulate, uneducated man' (Jack Hywel-Davies).

Leaders can even exploit their handicaps to advantage. Admiral Nelson once ignored an order by putting the telescope to his blind eye. He is famously quoted as saying, 'I have a right to be blind sometimes – I really do not see the signal,' thereby risking the wrath of his naval overlords.

Leaders have real authority

True authority cannot be limited to an unbroken tactile link to be traced back to St Peter. The New Testament contains no explicit record of a transmission of St Peter's leadership. Clearly authority comes directly from God whether in the church or the world (Romans 13:1). This then needs to be confirmed by the people recognising that this person clearly has God's authority to lead them. It was said of the explorer, Ernest Shackleton, that ultimately 'his authority rested on the genuine regard and respect of the men he led.'[15]

Authority in a leader's position should not be assumed

In today's world, the very definition of a leader is being transformed from someone whose authority is derived from the position held, to someone who has the human qualities necessary for building up an effective organisation, and to inspire outstanding individual performance. Does the leader take authority from God or does God give it to the leader? Is it God's anointing or man's appointing? It must be both.

No wise leaders will assume their authority by their mere

appointment, though every leader, when they take up office is usually credited with a certain amount of authority from their people 'like cash in the bank' (Steve Nicholson). Such credit is conceded with the job. But this may be soon eroded by futile bungling, unpopular appointments, unrealistic objectives or unrealised predictions. Such are enough to disenchant any followers. On the other hand increased authority will be credited to a leader by obvious effectiveness and beneficial achievements that have encouraged and inspired his/her followers.

Followers willingly extend authority to leaders (whom they assumed have been called by God) when they see caring commitment, integrity, ability, and benefits all round issuing out of their leadership.

Once authority has been generally granted from a committed following, leaders find themselves increasingly empowered by God ('For whosoever hath, to him shall be given, and he shall have more abundance' Matthew 13:12 KJV) to make things happen – so long as they maintain a humble and dependent relationship on God.

Leaders understand the significance of prayer

It is said that God is only a prayer away. No reader of the Gospels can but be impressed by the number of references to Jesus praying, both short utterances and long nights in prayer. Indeed his disciples were so impressed that they begged him to teach them how to pray (Luke 11:1). Spiritual authority is further endorsed and enhanced as the leader seeks God's presence – standing in God's counsel (Jeremiah 23:18) – listens to and obeys God's voice, and understands one's people.

Leaders understand the need for accountability

'A lot of leaders have catchy slogans on their desk; many believe in them,' wrote Rudolph Giuliani, a former mayor of New York. 'The two-word sign on my desk genuinely summarises my whole philosophy: I'M RESPONSIBLE. Throughout my career, I've maintained that accountability – the idea that the people who work for me are answerable to those we work for is the cornerstone. And the principle starts with me.'

More than anyone, leaders should welcome being held accountable, and it should be made plain from the start to whom they are accountable. Nothing builds confidence in a leader more than a willingness to take responsibility for what happens during his watch. One might add that nothing builds a stronger case for holding employees to a high standard than leaders who hold themselves to an even higher one. This is true in any organisation, but it's particularly important in a government or a church. A slogan on the desk of President Truman in the White House showed he knew his responsibility. It ran, 'The buck stops here.' Leaders need to remind themselves of this and never appear to be trying to wriggle out of it.

Leaders understand they are responsible

After a famous victory a French General was once tactlessly asked if the credit for it should not go to his second-in-command. The general pondered in silence for a little while before answering. 'Maybe so!' he said. 'But one thing is certain. If the battle had gone the other way I would have been blamed for losing it!'

Leaders understand the need of influence

The Italian word for influence is influenza, which was introduced into the English language in the mid-18th century, apparently adopted from the Italian term *influenza di freddo* (influence of the cold). Good leaders are contagious people. Their influence is caught contagiously like a disease. After the first Pentecost the Jewish Council in Jerusalem was increasingly worried about the rapid growth of converts to Jesus through the fearless preaching of the first disciples. They decided to oppose it saying, 'So that it [the good news of the kingdom of God] spreads no further among the people [like a contagious disease], let us severely threaten them, that from now on they speak to no man in this name [of Jesus]' (Acts 4:17 NKJV). Effective leaders are people of influence for better or for worse. Good leaders gain increasing influence by good leadership.

The road less travelled

Two roads diverged in a wood, and I
 – I took the one less travelled by,
And that has made all the difference.
                    (Robert Frost, *The Road Not Taken*)

A short course of leadership
The six most important words:
  'I admit I made a mistake.'
The five most important words:
  'I am proud of you.'
The four most important words:
  'What is your opinion?'
The three most important words:
  'If you please.'
The two most important words:
  'Thank you'
The least most important word:
  'I'

                    (J. Adair, *Effective Leadership*)

Prayer for leaders
    We thank you, God our Father,
    That from the days of the apostles,
    you have chosen men and women
    to exercise oversight in the Church,
    to guard its faith and guide its life.
    And to extend the kingdom of God.
    We pray for those who in our own day
    are called, or are being called, to leadership.
    May they follow the example of the apostles
    and obey you with holy and humble hearts.
    May they be strong and courageous in spirit.
    May they be listening to your voice and be preachers of your
      word.
    May they ever lift up the Cross of Jesus.
    May they build up the flock.
    May they train and equip new leaders
    in the teaching 'once delivered to the saints',
    And may they perceive and bless the new ways in which you
      are leading your Church today.
    For the extension of your kingdom and the glory of our
      Saviour Jesus Christ. Amen.

CHAPTER 2

People who worship

'And you shall be to Me a kingdom of priests and a holy nation'
(EXODUS 19:6 NKJV).

*'You are a chosen generation, a royal priesthood, a holy nation,
His own special people, that you may proclaim the praises
of Him who called you*
(1 PETER 2:9 NKJV).

*The first question in the Westminster Catechism is
'What is the chief end of man?'
Answer: 'Man's chief end is to glorify God
and to enjoy him for ever.'*

*Therefore praise not merely expresses, but completes the enjoyment.
In commanding us to glorify him,
God is inviting us to enjoy him.*
(C. S. LEWIS)

Church leaders are people who worship – 'We who first hoped in Christ have been destined and appointed to live for the praise of his glory' (Ephesians 1:12 RSV). They are also called to oversee worship for the congregations they lead. Those who direct the singing, instrumentalists, dance or drama are under their direct authority. Worship is fundamentally a meaningful encounter with the Lord God, Father, Son and Holy Spirit.

Matt Redman has said, 'The songs are nothing – it [worship] goes way beyond the music. It's our whole approach. Are we preparing our hearts for a divine encounter?'

Worship – mysterious divine encounter

A major obstacle for worship is our image of God. It is impossible for the mind of man to ever comprehend all the truth about God. He is incomprehensible. Most of his being, his will and his ways are past finding out. The preacher of righteousness underlines the limits of our knowledge, 'He has set eternity in their hearts yet they cannot fathom what God has done from beginning to end' (Ecclesiastes 3:11). However we can know some of the great things that God has done for us. But in the final analysis 'being past finding out' is just what we would expect of a God who is all-powerful, all-wise, omnipresent, omniscient, infinite and eternal. And no wonder such a God requires our worship!

God is full of *mysteries*. Five come immediately to mind.

1. The mystery of the Trinity.

Our God is three in one and one in three – three persons in one God – Father, Son and Holy Spirit. The trinity is never reasoned in Scripture but it is certainly revealed there. We are called to worship the holy unity of three persons – God the Father, God the Son and God the Holy Spirit; a holy fellowship into which all believers are gathered in a divine encounter of adoration and praise.

2. The mystery of God's transcendence and immanence

'Transcendence means that God is always greater, always beyond our imagining, separate and altogether different from his creation. He is also immanent, in all things.'[1] St Augustine is quoted as saying that God is 'Closer to man than I am to myself'. He is up and out there – and yet with, and in us down here. To overstress one side and overlook the other can lead us into all sorts of misconceptions and misrepresentations of God – indeed into heresy.

3. The mystery of the incarnation

Jesus was fully human whilst still being fully God. He had a truly human body and a rational soul (all that was characteristic of fallen man was found in him): in this sense he was the second Adam. And yet he possessed the Divine nature in its fullest sense. He was pre-existant (he was before all things). He was involved in the creation (without him was not anything made that was made) - and he is eternal. He was not two persons but one. His two natures were united in one personality. He said 'I and my Father are one.' (John 10:30)

4. The mystery of God's predestination and our free will

God is revealed to us as carefully working out his divine plan for us in Christ. God has foreknowledge of the future and elects us to eternal life. Mankind is predestined '... according to his purpose. For those whom he foreknew he also predestined ...' (Romans 8:28b,29a RSV).

But God has not chosen mankind to bow before him, kneel, dance and sing at his bidding like puppets on a string. He has given us the dignity of free will to choose to believe in him and serve him. 'I have set before you life and death, blessing and cursing; therefore choose life.' (Deuteronomy 30:19 NKJV) 'For God so loved the world that He gave His only begotten Son that whoever believes in Him should not perish but have everlasting life.' (John 3:16 NKJV) Mankind may choose whom or what to worship. We are not robots divinely programmed to worship God – we choose to worship him freely from the heart. This is all so clear, yet so enigmatic and irrational. Though God operates rationally he also operates supra-rationally. To cycle using one pedal will not keep the bicycle moving – to row with one oar will never get the boat to the other side of the river. We have to live with the paradox that we are predestined yet, at the same time, we have free will to choose. And never over-emphasise one truth at the expense of the other.

5. The mystery of God being both perfect love and a fearful consuming fire

But such is the God of the Bible that we worship.

(a) God is love (1 John 4:8b). God has clearly demonstrated his love for the world (John 3:16). Understanding such love compels us to draw near to God in worship, 'Because thy steadfast love is better than life, my lips will praise thee' (Psalm 63:3 RSV). The God we worship is – 'tender and compassionate, slow to anger, most loving' (Psalm 103:8).

(b) God is also the most Holy One, before whom Moses quaked with exceeding fear (Deuteronomy 9:19; Hebrews 12:21). It is only by his mercies that we are not consumed,

(Lamentations 3:22). We may not preach fire and brimstone much these days but the wrath of God, the awesome side of his nature, is still a serious reality that every true worshipper must acknowledge. 'Let us serve God acceptably, with reverence and awe ... our God is a consuming fire' (Hebrews 12:28,29).

The fact that many more mysteries are yet to be revealed to us about the Lord our God, does not prevent us from worshipping him for all the wonderful things already revealed about him. 'The secret things belong to the LORD our God, but those things which are revealed belong to us and to our children for ever' (Deuteronomy 29:29 NKJV).

TEMPLE MODEL FOR WORSHIP

In the Old Testament the people of Israel were taught to worship through the sacrificial rituals of the Tabernacle, through a particular form of priesthood and even from the fashioning and position of the furnishings. In this way a strong sense of God's holiness and awe was communicated. And it was all reproduced later within the Temple worship at Jerusalem under King Solomon. His father, King David, (the sweet psalmist of Israel, 2 Samuel 23:1), and other worship leaders, had also given Israel a liturgy of psalms which reflected God's greatness and mankind's fallenness, and taught the worshippers the place of repentance, thanksgiving, praise, prayer and sacrifice. The Old Testament also made provision for festivals, celebration and spontaneity.

There are three Biblical words for worship – two in the Old Testament and one in the New: the Hebrew word *hishahawah* meaning literally 'a bowing down' – prostration before God; the Hebrew word *aboda* meaning service, for which the Greek equivalent is *latreia*, the 'offering of ourselves' to God as a token of our submission, and recognition of his worth and honour.

The Greek word *proskunein* (John 4:24) is the most commonly used word for worship in the New Testament appearing 66 times, conveying the idea of 'coming towards to kiss'.

EARLY CHRISTIAN MODEL FOR WORSHIP

The New Testament church reflects some carry-over from the traditional Jewish worship models, the perennial feasts and some of the Temple rituals. The Last Supper was instituted in the context of the Passover celebration. Both Jesus and his disciples continued to worship on the Temple premises. The early Christians met together at Solomon's Porch (Acts 5:12).

There was also the current model of the synagogue where the first Christians met to worship regularly – when permitted by the local Jewish elders. This worship included Old Testament readings as well as teaching, praise and prayer, all carried over into the New Testament church.

Christian worship was born out of the fusion of Jewish temple worship, the annual festal celebrations, the synagogue gatherings, the Upper Room and Pentecost. They also had the Lord's Prayer. But beside the ritual and formality, was an element of spontaneity together with the manifestations of the Holy Spirit.

> Mary's *Magnificat* sprang from her lips when the Holy Spirit overshadowed her. Zechariah was filled with the Holy Spirit when he sang the *Benedictus*. Simeon's *Nunc Dimittis* came from one who had been guided by the Spirit into the temple at the time when the parents brought the child Jesus to it.[2]

This same freedom, openness and inspiration is anticipated in the post-Pentecostal church (1 Corinthians 14:26,27 and Ephesians 5:19,20), which was necessary if the gifts of the Spirit were not to be quenched.

In spite of the many details however, there is no full description or prescription of an early Christian service of worship. Possibly the clearest examples are of Paul's visit to Troas (Acts 20:7–12) and Paul's instructions to the Corinthian church (1 Corinthians 11;12;14).

HEAVEN'S MODEL FOR WORSHIP

In the book of Revelation heaven's curtain is drawn back and marvellous worship scenarios are clearly revealed to us.

> And I beheld, and I heard the voice of many angels round about the throne and the beasts and the elders: and the number of them was ten thousand times ten thousand, and thousands of thousands; Saying with a loud voice, Worthy is the Lamb that was slain to receive power, and riches, and

wisdom, and strength, and honour, and glory, and blessing.

And every creature which is in heaven, and on the earth, and under the earth, and such as are in the sea, and all that are in them, heard I saying, Blessing, and honour, and glory, and power, be unto him that sitteth upon the throne, and unto the Lamb for ever and ever.

And the four beasts said, Amen. And the four and twenty elders fell down and worshipped him that liveth for ever and ever. (Revelation 5:11–14 KJV) (See also Revelation 7:9–11; 22:3b–5)

Four key New Testament words about the conduct of worship
We find four key words in the New Testament to guide us in our conduct of worship, two used by Jesus in discussion with the woman of Samaria – *spirit* and *truth* (John 4:24), and two by Paul to the rather disorderly church of Corinth – *decency* and *order* (1 Corinthians 14:40). Leaders must be careful not to quench the Spirit and to make certain that the truth (Scripture) is taught and the gifts are practiced in a manner fitting for the maintenance of order in the church.

Worship needs ordering
It is the leader's responsibility to ensure order in worship. But what kind of order should it be?

There is an order of death in the cemetery, where nothing is supposed to move, and an order for life in the nursery where everything seems to be moving, and things need to be lovingly directed and tidied up. Obviously it's the latter that is needed for 'doing' church. I like the way John Gunstone talks about it as – 'order in the midst of creativity'.[3]

In private before the Lord, we may feel free to carry out our devotions in ways that are appropriate to our temperament. There is no prescribed pattern for this, but order is called for in public worship, especially, as St Paul stresses, where the gifts of the Spirit such as prophecy and tongues are freely encouraged (1 Corinthians 14:40). There is no set order, but a spontaneous directing, requiring a sensitivity that does not quench the Spirit. I picture the directing as that of a sensitive orchestral conductor, far removed from the domineering spirit of the sergeant major.

Worship needs time

To engage with God and meet with him in an intimate way takes time. The same is, of course, true of any relationship. To interact fully even with a close friend, or a marriage partner, doesn't just happen in a few quickly snatched moments. And yet in some churches, the service is rushed through with little thought of meeting with God. Surely the hope should be that the congregation will meet with the Lord in a direct and personal way. We need to come gradually, humbly and reverently into his presence. In this way people's hearts and minds can be fixed on God.[4]

WORSHIP NORMALLY INCLUDES TEN BASIC INGREDIENTS

Worship at any given time is usually made up from most of the following ingredients:

1. Faith

A worshipper must be a believer. 'He that cometh to God must believe that he is, and that he is a rewarder of them that diligently seek him' (Hebrews 11:6 KJV). The believer has come to faith in Jesus Christ as Lord and Saviour, whether this conversion came suddenly through a blinding light or gradually like the creeping dawn. In some way s/he has been born again and now knows God the Father through Jesus Christ, and has assurance of this. 'The Spirit Himself bears witness with our spirit that we are children of God' (Romans 8:16 NKJV).

2 Confession

True worshippers are very aware of their unworthiness in the light of God's holiness and feel bound to confess their sins, 'Day and night thy hand was heavy upon me ... I acknowledge my sin unto thee, and mine iniquity have I not hid. I said, I will confess my transgressions unto the Lord.' (Psalm 32:4,5 KJV) 'Woe is me! for I am undone.' (Isaiah 6:5 KJV) 'Depart from me; for I am a sinful man, O Lord' (Luke 5:8 KJV).

These are all familiar verbal responses arising from encounters with God.

3. Meditation
This activity of the mind has been likened to a horse mulling over his oats. The worshipper mulls over the Word of God with others when gathered together, and over God's creation when scattered abroad – over Scripture and nature, God's Word and God's works. This dimension of worship is not usually regulated by a fixed time limit or cultivated through any particular system.

4. Wonderment
'Worship thrives on wonder' (Matt Redman). God's judgements are unsearchable and his ways are past finding out (Romans 11:33). We stand in amazement before the mysteries of God.

5. Praise
Knowing God as the Creator, worshippers want to express their praise for all of creation. Such praising can be through singing – psalms, hymns and spiritual songs (including singing in tongues). Knowing God as the Redeemer worshippers desire to praise him for such love, mercy and grace.

6. Thanksgiving
Appreciation for how much has been received compels the true worshipper to thank God for all his goodness and loving kindness to us and to everyone.

7. Adoration
'O come let us adore him!' Worship is seeking to touch the heart of God with our love, and abandoning our wills to his will. The believer spends time in God's presence seeking God's face (Psalm 27:8). 'I have sought your face with all my heart' (Psalm 119:58 NIV). The believer delights in the beauty of the Lord (Psalm 27:4).

8. Prayer, intercession
Part of worship involves praying and interceding. It shows that we look to God for help in time of need. It shows we believe in his power to provide. Believing that God cares for us and the world's oppressed and needy, there will be a desire to spend time in prayer and intercession. (I Timothy 2:1-3)

9. Sacrifice

When David wanted to buy Araunah's threshing place, Araunah offered it free. David answered:

> 'No, but I will surely buy it from you for a price; nor will I offer burnt offerings to the LORD ... with that which costs me nothing.' So David bought the threshing floor and the oxen for fifty shekels of silver (2 Samuel 24:24 NKJV).

In the Temple worship there were prescriptions for the sacrifices of bulls, sheep, goats, birds and grain etc. For the worshipper to offer something costly represented a genuine commitment to God. In the New Testament Paul highlights this aspect on many occasions:

> '... present your bodies a living sacrifice, holy, acceptable to God, which is your reasonable service' (Romans 12:1 NKJV).

> '... they first gave themselves to the Lord, and then to us ...'(2 Corinthians 8:5 NKJV).

> 'Now concerning the collection for the saints ... On the first day of the week let each one of you lay something aside, storing up as he may prosper, that there be no collections when I come' (1 Corinthians 16:1,2 NKJV).

> 'Let him who is taught the word share in all good things with him who teaches. Do not be deceived. God is not mocked; for whatever a man sows, that he will also reap ... Therefore, as we have opportunity, let us do good to all, especially to those who are of the household of faith' (Galatians 6:6,7,10 NKJV).

> 'But as you abound in everything – in faith, in speech ... see that you abound in this grace [of giving] also' (2 Corinthians 8:7 NKJV).

> 'God loves a cheerful giver' (2 Corinthians 9:7 NKJV).

Matt Redman has said,

We do well in our worship to ask the same question as the boy Isaac once asked, 'Where's the sacrifice?' Sometimes in our meetings the 'fire' and the 'wood' are there – in other words, outwardly everything seems to be in place and we think we are set for 'great worship'. But something is missing: 'where's the sacrifice?'

10. Obedience

King Saul was disobeying God but thought he could keep God satisfied by offering sacrifices. The prophet Samuel rebuked him in God's name and reminded him that 'to obey is better than to sacrifice' (1 Samuel 15:22 NKJV) and Jesus says in John 15:14 (NKJV), 'You are My friends if you do whatever I command you.' Sometimes God speaks to us about specific things but there is always a general lifestyle requirement where our commitment is called for: 'What doth the LORD require of thee, but to do justly, to love mercy, and to walk humbly with thy God' (Micah 6:8).

Dimensions of worship

Worship has its *emotional, spiritual, doctrinal* and *physical* dimensions. Jesus summarised the Ten Commandments given to Moses in Mark 12:30 (NIV), 'Love the Lord your God with all your heart and with all your soul and with all your mind and with all your strength.'

Worship develops into set liturgy

Sooner or later any congregation develops its own set liturgy if it does not already have one, so in experimenting we have a duty to ensure that it's a wholesome and God-honouring one. And because other Christians will worship with us from time to time, it is sensible and considerate to have some liturgical commonality that will help them to participate and feel at home.

The Christian church has a storehouse of rich liturgical expression stretching back 3,000 years. Much of it may be wordy, too quaint and old fashioned, or too long, but some is short, succinct, simple, beautiful, profound, appropriate for our times and edifying. An old Pentecostal pastor expressed his delight recently when he discovered the *Book of Common Prayer* (1662) and realised how this dimension in worship had eluded him during his ministry.

It may be unwise in some settings to use too much liturgy but it would be equally unwise to ignore it completely, especially when home-produced liturgies can be wordy, repetitive, ill-phrased, carelessly expressed, and grammatically confusing, and I have to say, even boring. They can soon become as predictable as any set liturgy and often much less edifying. Choose wisely but keep a choice selection available by the lectern (and printed out for the leader and for the overhead screen).

The same applies with the sacraments, for confirmations, dedications, weddings, funerals, disposing of ashes, and blessings etc. Remember that the more dignified the setting, the more valued the treasure at the heart of it. The more beautiful the ring of gold, the more glorious the central diamond.

QUOTES

- The glory of God is a living man; and the life of a man consists in beholding God. (St Irenaeus)
- Worship, then, is not part of the Christian life; it is the Christian life. (Gerald Vann)
- When we come to worship we come to a throne … and everything else arranges itself around that throne. (Rowan Williams)
- It is only when men begin to worship that they begin to grow. (Calvin Coolridge)
- Worship is rendering to God that of which he is worthy. (Eric L. Mascall)
- Worship depends not upon our own activities, but upon the activities which God brings to bear upon us; to them we are forced to react as worshippers. (Kenneth E. Kirk)
- God does not depend upon our worship (Psalm 50:12; Acts 17:25), though his very nature demands it. (Anon)
- Accustom yourself, then, by degrees thus to worship him to beg his grace, to offer him your heart from time to time in the midst of your business, even every moment if you can. Do not always scrupulously confine yourself to certain rules, or particular forms of devotion, but act with a general confidence in God, with love and humility. (Brother Lawrence 1611–91)
- O my God! If I worship Thee from fear of hell, burn me in hell, and if I worship Thee from hope of Paradise, exclude

me from it; but if I worship Thee for Thine own sake, then withhold not from me Thine Eternal Beauty. (Rabia Al-Aadawiyya)

- Adoration begins when we are captivated by the living God – not for what he does or promises, but just for who he is … There is much worship that stops short of adoration. In doing so it remains on the level of appreciation or another way of offering thanks to God. But adoration is not appreciation but *abandonment* – abandonment before the wonder and beauty of God in all his glory. (David Runcorn)

- Worship is the submission of our nature. It is the quickening of conscience by his holiness; the nourishment of the mind with his truth; the purifying of imagination with his beauty, the opening of the heart to his love; the surrender of the will to his purpose – and all gathered up in adoration. (Archbishop William Temple)

- Worship is the people of God travelling home. (Robert M. E. Paterson)

- Christian worship is the most momentous, the most urgent, the most glorious action that can take place in human life. (Karl Barth)

- Worship is the dramatic celebration of God in his supreme worth in such a manner that his 'worthiness' becomes the norm and inspiration of human living. (Ralph P. Martin)

- *Leiturgia* is a service offered by God's people to the Father through Jesus Christ – a gift of corporate prayer and praise in response to God's Word. (John Gunstone)

- *Leitourgia* or worship is, first of all, offering praise, thanksgiving and adoration to God, but it is also a powerful witness to the world. The New Testament clearly recognises the significance of worship for witness. (Michael Nazir-Ali), (eg 1 Corinthians 14:25)

- Worship is the highest form of spiritual warfare. (Lois Gott)

- Some of God's attributes are too wonderful to understand. But even if they remain darkness to the intellect, let them be sunshine for your soul. (Anon)

- Tell me whom you love, and I will tell you who you are. (Houssaye)

- The best and most beautiful things in life cannot be seen or even touched … they must be felt with the heart. (Helen Keller, who was blind)
- If worship is mindless it is meaningless. (Rick Warren)
- Worship is to feel God in your heart. (A. W. Tozer)
- Every posture in worship says something of both the worshipper, and the one being glorified. (Matt Redman)
- Worship is the fuel for mission's flame … and worship is also the heart of mission's aim. (Matt Redman)
- Lord, you created me for yourself and my heart is restless until it rests in thee. (St Augustine)
- The first priority of any church leader is to have a full-time music director. (Rick Warren)
- The key word for any lead worshipper is 'anointed'. (Anon)

ILLUSTRATIONS
Ways of Drawing Near to God
Gary Grant has identified nine ways people are inclined to draw near to God.

Naturalists are most inspired to love God out of doors in natural settings.

Sensates love God with their senses and appreciate beautiful worship services that involve their sight, taste, smell, and touch, not just their ears.

Traditionalists draw closer to God through rituals, liturgies, symbols and unchanging structures.

Ascetics prefer to love God in solitude and simplicity.

Activists love God though confronting evil, battling injustice, and working to make the world a better place.

Caregivers love God by loving others and meeting their needs.

Enthusiasts love God through celebration.

Contemplatives love God through adoration.

Intellectuals love God by studying with their minds[5] 'They know their hearts will never fully engage until their minds are filled with truth.' (Bill Hybels)

Believers usually develop along one mode at first and then, as time goes by, begin to experience other approaches also. Not all modes help everyone. We should not be over critical with ourselves if we don't always like this or that approach. Bill Hybels tells the story[6] of 'a pastor who used to beat himself up mercilessly for not spending enough time in solitude. Strange thing though, whenever he did manage to be alone for long periods of time, he became brooding and morose. Dark thoughts filled his mind. Though he engaged in solitude to make himself available to God, the experience never failed to set him back spiritually!' We are all so different. For some, the hearty Charismatic approach is too threatening. A Catholic approach seems too theatrical. A Quaker approach may seem too silent. An Evangelical approach is sometimes too lifeless!

Renewals can soon become formalised

Most Anglo-Catholics have been brought up in a tradition that liked drama, colour, lights, movement, bells and smells. This 'renewal' had started as a reaction to ways in which worship was conducted in many evangelical churches in the 1830s, often joyless, colourless and lifeless.

One former Anglo-Catholic has described how for him the most important thing about liturgy was that it should be done 'decently and in order'. Certain things were traditional and tasteful and worthy of God; other things weren't. It was my job to uphold the former and banish the latter (though the criteria for deciding this were decidedly limited). I believed that if the Holy Spirit manifested himself to us as we worshipped, it was because we were doing everything according to the directions laid down in the liturgical manual in fashion at the time. So everybody who participated in the service – servers, organist, choir, readers, sidesmen – had to be drilled until they played their part correctly. If the reader stumbled over a difficult word, or one of the sidesmen started taking the collection during the wrong hymn, this spoilt the worship. It had not been a 'good service'.[7] (John Gunstone)

Comment from a leader's wife

George Carey relates how, when a church leader in Durham, his wife came out of their church and said 'I am not sure that I can put up with this diet – it is so boring!' Carey was forced to reflect on what they were doing. 'There we were in the heart of Durham with a style of worship which was lifeless and unattractive. I realised with a heavy heart that something had to be done ... Our worship is a shop window to the world. If our worship is attractive as well as reverend, joyful as well as devotional, relevant as well as anchored in Scripture, then God will use it to draw many to him. So with this philosophy before us we fashioned our services to express our love and worship of God.[8]

What does God think of our worship?

I was once chatting to the leader of a growing Christian fellowship in Honolulu, and his wife. This once struggling church on one of the Hawaiian islands had been passing through an oppressive period. The wife told how she had become so weighed down by the worship one Sunday morning that she left the church and went outside to pray. She began crying out to God. 'Lord what is wrong? What is wrong in there?' and almost immediately she began to sense the Lord was speaking to her and telling her to go back in. He had something he wanted her to do there. When she understood what it was she begged to be excused, but still God seemed to be insisting. So she answered 'Well, Lord, if my husband asks me to speak when I return [which he had never done in his life before] then I will know for sure I must do it for you.'

As she quietly re-entered her husband caught sight of her and, totally out of character, he called out, 'Have you come back with anything for us from the Lord?' Her heart sank. Now she knew she just had to do it. She nodded and moved directly to the centre of the church, and with a quick word of apology, she spat on the floor and cried out 'That's what God thinks of our worship!' In an instant the Spirit of God fell upon that congregation in a most extraordinary way – people slumped to the floor and wept in repentance. That day was a turning point in the life of their church. Obviously no one should ever try to repeat that, but we would all do well to ask ourselves, 'What does God really think of our worship? Does it please him? Does it touch his heart?'

African–American Worship

I attended a three-and-a-half-hour worship service at our neighbouring African-American church, which I love to be a part of. I was the last of nine pastors who spoke in celebration of the pastor's thirty-fourth anniversary in that ministry. They clapped a lot. My hands got numb. They swayed a lot. They said, 'Amen!' 'Yes!' 'All right!' 'Well, well!' 'Come on!' 'Say that here!' 'Bring it on home!' They sang very loud. They played the organ as background music to a couple of messages. They shouted. I loved it. I wish our church would learn a few things from them.[9] (John Piper)

Experience Abroad

I remember once, I was officiating at an Anglican commmmmunion service early on in my time in Chile. We had reached that part of the liturgy which ran 'Therefore with angels and archangels, and with all the company of heaven we laud and magnify thy glorious name, evermore praising thee and saying holy, holy, holy', when suddenly the whole congregation seemed to 'lift off', breaking out spontaneously into shouts and cries of Glory! Praise be to God! Hallelujah etc. It was both surprising and refreshing and I just let it run till there seemed an appropriate moment to continue. I mentally decided to omit a later set part of the service so as not to prolong things too much as I continued with the set service.

Credo

I believe in the sun
Even when it is not shining.
I believe in love
Even when I feel it not.
I believe in God
Even when He is silent
(Scribbled on a wall in a Nazi concentration camp)

Biblical quote

'How great are God's riches! How deep are his wisdom and knowledge! Who can explain his decisions? Who can understand his ways? ... For all things were created by him, and all things exist through him and for him. To God be the glory for ever! Amen' (Romans 11:33,34 GNB).

Leaders bid to worship

We have come together as the family of God in our Father's presence to offer Him praise and thanksgiving,
to hear and receive His holy word,
to bring before Him the needs of the world

to ask His forgiveness of our sins,
and to seek His grace,
that through His Son Jesus Christ
we may give ourselves to His service.
(ASB 1980)

Prayer
You are to be blessed and praised;
all good things come from you:
you are in our words and in our thoughts, and in all that we do.
Amen.
(St Teresa of Avila 1515–82)

Blessing
Now unto the King eternal, immortal, invisible, the only wise God,
be honour and glory for ever and ever, Amen.

CHAPTER 3

People who have vision

'He made known his ways unto Moses,
his acts unto the children of Israel'

(PSALM 103:7 KJV).

'According to all that I show you ... the pattern of the tabernacle ...
so you shall make it'

(EXODUS 25:9).

A great organisation has someone at the top saying 'This is where we
are going, this is what we stand for, this is what we believe in.'

(KEN BLANCHARD)

A blind man's world is bounded by the limits of his touch,
an ignorant man's world by the limits of his knowledge,
a great man's world by the limits of his vision.

(PAUL HARVEY)

If the vision tarries wait for it.

(HABAKKUK 2:3)

Vision is an effective leader's chief occupation.

(HANS FITZEL)

A major topic at leaders' seminars today is the 'V' word – Vision. We
remember how Martin Luther King inspired his followers with a
classic vision:

> I have been to the mountain top ... I've looked over and seen
> the Promised Land. I may not get there with you, but I want
> you to know tonight that we, as a people, will get to the

Promised Land. So I am happy tonight ... I'm not fearing man. 'Mine eyes have seen the glory of the coming of the Lord.'[1]

But getting the right vision can seem a rather elusive pursuit. Some leaders are frustrated and feel they are failures for never having a great vision from God, while others claim to have visions that seem weird, impracticable or clearly just self-centred. It would be easy, though irresponsible, to dismiss the whole idea. But vision creates faith and inspires hope. Vision provides new energy for the new efforts, fresh wisdom for its implementation and firmer resolve to endure the opposition that might ensue. Not all visionaries are leaders but all leaders should be visionaries. Jesus lamented over the Jewish hierarchy of his day; he called them 'blind leaders of the blind'. It seems they had no visionaries among them. Lack of vision has been defined as an 'ecclesiastical terminal illness'.[2] Too many church leaders have been playing at 'Blind Man's Buff' for too long – and when the blind lead the blind they all fall.

In the Old Testament vision often seems to have originated with the prophets. But there were prophets in Jeremiah's day, who missed the divine cues and were rebuked by God for prophesying without seeking a message from him, for not having first 'stood in my counsel' (Jeremiah 23:22). Once we become serious about our relationship with God, and listen to him, we will be surprised at how God begins to reveal his purposes and plans. When a boy falls in love with a girl, and starts spending all the time he can with her, he soon envisages the things that would please her, and longs to do them for her.

WHAT IS VISION?

Quite simply vision is seeing ahead. 'Vision is about reality yet to be. There is therefore a creative tension between what is and what will be.' (Robert Warren)

J. Oswald Sanders, a missionary statesman, and student of the Church worldwide, once wrote, 'Those who have most powerfully and permanently influenced their generation have been the "seers" – men and women who have seen more and further than the rest of us.' Like Moses they 'endured as seeing the invisible' (Hebrews 11:27). Moses could see what his followers could not see; he was a man of far horizons.

A SNAPSHOT OF THE FUTURE

'A vision is a picture of a future state for the organization, a descriptuion of what it would like to be in a number of years from now. It is a dynamic picture of the organization in the future, as seen by its leadership. It is more than a dream or set of hopes, becauase top management is demonstrably committed to its realization: it ios a committment.' (Richard Beckhart and Wendy Pritchard in *Changing the Essence*)

HOW CAN WE GET A VISION?

A God-given vision may be revealed through prophecy or a dream, especially after fasting and prayer. Or it might just come through sitting down alone, or with others, or by prayerfully considering whether this or that was a good idea.

And if a vision comes, how and when can it be achieved?

Visions often come through a profound dissatisfaction over the way things actually are, the prospect of an urgent need, the arrival of some sizeable gift, an increase of money or land, a significant growth in the church's membership, a sense that the church should be more involved in social justice or mission overseas – any one of these can lead to a compelling idea of the way things could be. What if we copied what we have seen elsewhere, maybe simply adjusting it to our particular church? Many good ideas arise out of this process. They suddenly appear to be the obvious missing pieces in the mosaic of God's mission where we are. Having said that, there are those who receive original visions much more than others.

IMAGINED POSSIBILITY

C. S. Lewis talked somewhere about 'baptised imagination'. Imagination handed over to God and 'soaked in the Spirit' may certainly be the pathway to vision. A close relationship to the Lord is the key for this exercise. In the introduction to his book, *The Liquid Church*, Pete Ward starts with a 'health warning'. 'Liquid church does not exist,' he says. 'This means that what I say here is an attempt to imagine rather than describe a different way of being church.'[3]

Simple imagination can play one of the biggest single parts in a leader's achievements. It has a powerful influence over life. We automatically move in the direction of our dominant thoughts.

Psychologists tell us that the human mind can sometimes hardly distinguish between things that happen in truth and things imagined in an atmosphere charged with emotional intensity. When we believe something to be true, we see the world in that way. Imagination allows us to explore what we consider to be reality in a completely new way and inspires us to act 'as if'.

LISTENING TO GOD WHEN VISION IS NEEDED
a. God speaks to us

Our God is not like those deaf and dumb idols that the pagans make and worship. Idols have ears, eyes and mouths but can neither hear, see, nor speak, whereas our God is a living God who speaks (cf Job 33:14; Psalm 19:1–4); and clearly God still wants to speak to our churches today (Rev. 2:7,11,17,29; 3:13,22). Jesus seemed to be seeking always to listen to his Father (John 5:19; 12:49,50), and he told his disciples to listen too.

'My sheep hear my voice.'
The sheep 'know his voice' (John 10:4).

From heaven God had commanded his hearers – '… This is my beloved Son … listen to him' (Matthew 17:5 RSV).

Of course, it is not uncommon for Christians, like King David before them, to feel sometimes that God is hiding from them (Psalms 10:1; 13:1,2; 28:1; 44:24), has withdrawn from them (Psalms 22:1,2; 38:21), and the heavens are keeping silent in response to their prayers (Psalm 109:1). That is simply a way by which God sometimes tests us to see if we still really trust him even when we can't see him, hear him or understand him (John 20:29).

b. Listening well requires silence

The best environment for listening is solitude and silence. King David obviously found nights a good time to listen to God. 'On my bed I remember you; I think of you through the watches of the night' (Psalm 63:6 NIV). Brother Lawrence managed to make the silences in his monastery kitchen, where he worked, a time for his soul to be lifted up above earthly things and held by God.

God sometimes takes us away from our familiar surroundings to a place of silence to gain our attention, when for some reason we have stopped trying to listen to him. He once said of rebellious Israel, 'I will lead her into the desert and speak tenderly to her' (Hosea 2:14 NIV). At times he even allows us to pass through suffering to compel us to listen.

C. S. Lewis has called pain God's megaphone. In our afflictions God often comes through, whether we want to hear him or not. It is quite amazing how hard and callous our hearts can become as the Old Testament prophets sadly observed. 'My people stubbornly refused to listen. They closed their minds and made their hearts as hard as rock … Because they did not listen when I spoke, I did not answer when they prayed' (Zechariah 7:11–13 GNB). After many remarkable signs and wonders in the wilderness, the children of Israel still had times when they refused to listen to him. God has warned us not to follow their dangerous example (Psalm 95:8).

But the general rule is that if we draw near to God he will draw near to us (James 4:8).

c. Hearing and obeying God makes the difference

Moses had grown up in Pharaoh's palace, believing that he could, one day, help his own people because of his privileged position. (His Israeli mother would probably have told him that he had been saved from the river for such a time as this!) Then everything seemed to go wrong after he killed an Egyptian who was fighting with an Israelite. Moses had to escape for his life into the desert where he settled down to the humdrum role of a Bedouin shepherd. There he married a woman who did not seem to have been totally sympathetic with his religious faith (Exodus 4:24–26). No doubt after all those years Moses felt that he had forfeited all his chances of doing anything useful for them and had settled for second best. How many church leaders would identify with him?

Then one day on the 'backside of the desert' something caught his attention – a bush aflame! Desert people occasionally see cases of spontaneous combustion when some prickly agave goes up in black smoke. Moses might easily have passed it by. But his curiosity was aroused and he thought, 'I must just go and take a look!' God then called Moses from out of the burning bush, called him to be the greatest human leader (apart from Jesus), the world has ever known!

Had Moses not heard, or had he disobeyed God, then Israel

might never have been liberated, nor entered the promised land of 'milk and honey'. Moses' life-changing vision became the people's life-long provision and salvation.

OTHERS GET VISIONS TOO

The availability of certain gifted people in any church may also help in the capture of visions. Asked how he made so many discoveries, Sir Isaac Newton replied that he had been able to see farther than other people because he had been standing on the shoulders of giants. Not all visions have to originate with the leader. They can also come from members of the church or from outsiders, from reading books or from visiting other places.

GOD'S NEW THINGS

God is always doing new things (Isaiah 43:19) and we need to be ready – discerning enough, sensitive enough, and seeking enough to hear his voice or see his visions whenever he wants to reveal them. Of course, it's not always quite that easy. In his book, *Alone With God*, Richard Wurmbrand, who spent fourteen lonely years of torture and starvation in a Communist prison cell for his Christian faith, once wrote, 'I pray for a time and then just listen. From immeasurable Satanic depths fiery darts are thrown at the soul'.[4] We all struggle one way or another in drawing near to God.

No two leaders are the same – their strengths and personalities differ; their gifts and weaknesses differ. No two churches are the same. Their congregations and circumstances differ. God leads different leaders and different churches in different ways at different times and gives them differing visions.

There is no way of determining exactly how, when, why or where people are going to receive visions, but we may remind ourselves of Brother Yun, a modern leader of the House Church Movement in China, who also suffered excruciating torture for his faith, but was given many remarkable revelations which affected his ministry significantly. He writes,

Let me take a moment to explain what it's like when I receive a dream or a vision from the Lord. These don't happen frequently, but usually when there is something important or urgent God wants to impress on me. All the visions I've received are very short, often lasting just a second or two. Often a picture or a scene flashes into my spirit and mind, yet it is so vivid and real I know it's from the Lord.[5]

As Christians, however, we are not to live for visions or dreams, nor should we inordinately seek after them. We live to seek the Lord himself and live by his Word. But we should at all times be open to the Lord speaking to us in any way and at anytime he chooses. This includes the revelation of himself to us through dreams and visions.

Of course, any such revelation we receive must be carefully weighed against the Scriptures. Nothing from God will ever counter the touchstone of his inspired Word. God does not contradict himself.

RECOGNIZING A COMMUNICATION HANG-UP
A gentleman was walking down a residential street and noticed a man struggling with a washing machine at the doorway of his house. When he volunteered to help, the homeowner was overjoyed and the two men together began to struggle with the bulky appliance. After several minutes of fruitless effort the two stopped and just looked at each other. They were on the verge of exhaustion. Finally, when they caught their breath, the man said to the homeowner 'We'll never get this washing machine in there!' To which the homeowner replied 'In? I'm trying to move it out!'

CASTING A VISION
The way in which a vision is communicated and its timing is very important. We have to get the vision across somehow, if it concerns the church. The first essential before casting the vision is to clarify it. David Watson has warned, 'Make sure that what you want to achieve are God's objectives and not your own fancies.' Once the vision is put into words it will be in the open where the people can see it, agree with it, pray about it, criticise it and fine-tune it.

But whatever its origin it will never be taken up by the local church if the leaders do not *own* it themselves, and are not clearly seen to be right behind it. If they have doubts, so will the church. If they have fears, so will the organisation. Also in order to inspire and persuade followers, the visions must be both responsible and realistic, never naïve or simply idealistic.

Discussing the Labour Party, Michael Wills, an ex-cabinet minister, wrote, 'We have to find a better way of expressing our ideological vision. I don't think people understood what the Third Way was … in terms of a positive vision, a shining city on the hill – it never persuaded.'

Leaders must understand what is needed to persuade their people – how it can be made to work profitably. The vision will have no relevance unless it can be imparted clearly to those who need to capture it. Leaders must ensure that the vision is communicated by someone in the church – preferably by the leaders themselves, and certainly in their presence – in a way that most attracts and excites those concerned. An Arabian proverb says, 'He is the best speaker who can turn the ear into an eye.'

So that the vision can be captured four vital areas need to be covered:

1. the relevant facts about the vision;
2. the form, or programme it will take (with some prepared sketches or models) to demonstrate how it will work;
3. the positive results that are to be expected;
4. a plan for financing it.

All this needs to be communicated in simple compelling statements.

Leaders need to exercise great care in how they communicate their visions to their public. If the prophecies fail to match the predictions, leaders undermine their own authority and leave their people fearing that their leaders' word is untrustworthy. Rudolph Giuliani has remarked that 'Grand rhetorical promises undermine a leader's authority.' Do not try to communicate your vision too soon. Be well prepared for its presentation so that people will be well prepared to receive it. 'A premature announcement of what you are going to do unsettles potential supporters, gives opponents time to construct real and imaginary defences and tends to ensure failure.'[6]

This means clearly spelling out how you get to where you want to go. A company Executive Officer has said, 'I play the visionary role and I have to be like a third grade teacher in communicating it. I say it over and over until people get it right, right, right.'

QUOTES

- When left in the dark people tend to dream up wild rumours. (Hans Finzel)
- Where there is no vision, the people perish. (Proverbs 29:18 KJV).
- Were there is no vision the people are unrestrained. (Bill Hybels)
- Where there is only vision the people have nervous breakdowns. (Leonard Sweet)
- We all live under the same sky but we don't all have the same horizons. (Conrad Audenauer)
- Traditional leaders are driven by heritage. Apostolic leaders are driven by vision. (Peter Wagner)
- Imagination is nothing more than the ability to make images. (Anon)
- Expect great things from God. Attempt great things for God. (William Carey)
- What could be worse than being born without sight? Being born with sight and having … no vision. (Helen Keller, who was physically blind but certainly had vision)
- Reaching goals is fine for an annual plan. Only reaching one's potential is fine for a life. (Max Depree)
- Vision creates faith and inspires hope. (David Pytches)
- I find that the constant inspiration of looking at the goal is the chief thing that helps me to persevere. (Douglas Thornton, Christian Mission Leader in Egypt)
- Some people see things as they are and ask 'Why?' I like to see things as they are not and ask 'Why not?' (George Bernard Shaw)
- You ask, what is our aim? I can answer in one word: it is victory, victory at all costs, victory in spite of terror, victory however long and hard the road may be. (W. S. Churchill)
- In life, as in football, you won't go far unless you know where the goalposts are. (Anon)
- Every true life has its Jerusalem to which it is always going up. (Phillip Brooks)
- Without a vision you lose elections.[7] (Insightful headline)
- When we pray coincidences happen: when we don't, they don't.' (William Temple)

- Two men looked out from prison bars, one saw mud, the other stars. (Anon)
- Lord I am coming as fast as I can. (Archbishop Laud)
- Expectations for how a vision will have grown in the first year are usually far too high; expectations for how much it will have grown in five years are usually far too low. (Anon)
- Without vision people die. (Elaine Storkey)
- Church leaders cannot blindly follow the path charted by people who operate on a different world view. (George Barna)
- Vision is the key to the vitality of thriving churches. (Bill Hybels)
- Vision is at the very core of leadership. (Bill Hybels)
- We have to wait for the vision. (Robert Warren)
- Articulating the vision may be the single most important responsibility that a leader has. (Walter Wright)

ILLUSTRATIONS
The old prophet type
Another kind of religious leader must arise among us. He must be the old prophet type, a man who has seen visions of God and has heard a voice from the Throne (A. W. Tozer).

> Never ascribe to God what is not of God. Do not suppose too easily that dreams, voices, impressions, visions, revelations, are from God without sufficient evidence. They could be purely natural, they may be diabolical. Test all things by the Scriptures. When it comes from God it comes with profound impact and makes an unforgettable impression.

A person in despair
Everything had gone wrong for Graham Pulkingham, the rector of the Church of the Redeemer in Houston, Texas.

> 'I was in despair. Everything that was offered had been despised, and finally the church withdrew ... I took the burden of it into a lonely basement chapel which, for six weeks from Ash Wednesday to Easter, became my tomb of

despair.

It was in that lonely chapel during Lent that I became a visionary. There revelations I received were not flights of fancy or mere daydreams, nor were they conclusions drawn. from a rapidly reasoned processes ... In the unveiling of two stark future moments I visualized a church of Eastwood as it was to be – a loving, sharing, serving, community of praise and thanksgiving, and I saw the ministry, or more personally my own ministry as it was to be ... it involved a mysterious endowment of power to impart life for death, health for sickness, and freedom for bondage.'[8]

A picture of the next step

Some years ago I visited a church in Kansas City led by Mike Bickle, that had outgrown its space and were praying about the need of a new facility. A prophetic member of their church gave them a picture of the place and its location, which he felt that God had shown him. It was to be conveniently built on an intersection in town but a major feature was the stretch of green grass that the prophet saw on which it seemed to be built. Naturally the church members scoured the city to find a green swathe of grass near an intersection in the city where they might possibly be able to build. They found absolutely nothing.

Meanwhile the pressure to move grew. One day they had a visit from a couple of businessmen who had a facility which they thought would be ideal for the congregation and wanted Mike Bickle to go and see. If he liked it the church could have the use of it at a very low rent. It was tempting, but Mike, wanting God's will, had his heart set on the place that God had earmarked for them, which had been clearly described by the prophet. Reluctant to waste their time but thinking it might be a pro tem solution he accepted their invitation.

They found a large building built conveniently near an intersection of roads, and on entering discovered the whole place carpeted with plastic green grass. The building had originally been designed to be a Sports Centre but had never proved itself financially viable. Mike Bickle was could see it was the very place that God had intended for them all along.

LAY FOLK HAVE VISIONS TOO

What a loss to never hear a timid member say with Spirit-prompted boldness, 'I know this sounds like a crazy idea, but what if we …' What a loss never to look around the circle as eyes light up, bodies lean forward, and a team member says 'What a fantastic idea!'… And then later when someone says, 'Do you remember when God broke through? Do you remember when that idea was born? Can you believe all that happened since then? Can you believe we got to do this together?'

Those are holy moments, moments that bring you to your knees in thanksgiving for what God has done through the ragtag team of which you are a part. No leader should miss these moments.[9]

VISIONS DO NOT HAVE TO BE ORIGINAL

'I'm not a great inventor,' protested Thomas A. Edison to a State Governor.

'But you have over a thousand patents to your credit!' said the Governor.

'Yes, but the only invention I can really claim as absolutely original is the phonograph,' replied Edison.

'But I don't understand you.'

'Well,' Edison explained, 'I guess I'm an awfully good sponge. I absorb ideas from every source I can, and then put them to practical use. Then I improve them until they become of some value. The ideas I use are mostly the ideas of other people who do not develop them.'

VISION NEEDS THE LEADER'S OWNERSHIP

We once had a magnificent vision for a vital extension in our church at St Andrew's, Chorleywood, which would cost many thousands of pounds. Whilst I was convinced we needed the new development and the plans were good, yet I was still a little unsure about taking it to the church because, to the best of my knowledge, they had never had to raise such an amount before. It was such a relief when Fred Evans, our treasurer, simply sketched how he could see the money coming in. He broke the total down to blocks of £25,000, £10,000, £5,000, £2,000, £1,000, £500, £100 and £50 showing how many we would need if the gifts were large and how the total sum could quite possibly be reached with smaller gifts or loans. Suddenly I could see it all coming in. The vision had been easily communicated to me and could easily be conveyed to the church – the building extension was needful and the expectation for raising the money was realistic.

VISION EVOKES SUPPORT
The man with the vision met the man with the money
The man with the money got the vision
The man with the vision got the money.

TRUSTING THE VISIONARY
The famous evangelist once asked a little boy the way to the nearest post office. When the lad explained it to him, Billy Graham thanked him and said, 'If you come to the convention centre tonight you can hear me telling everyone how to get to heaven.'

'No thanks,' said the boy. 'You don't even know the way to the post office!'

COMMUNICATING VISION
Winston Churchill, one of the greatest British prime ministers of all time, is remembered for giving the lion's roar during the threat of German invasion at the beginning of the Second World War. His speeches not only expressed defiant resolve, but they rallied an ill prepared and poorly equipped island nation to believe Hitler's attacks could be repelled. One of his broadcasts at a most critical time in 1940 still inspires people today:

> You ask what is our policy? I will say it is to wage war, by sea, land, and air, with all our might and all the strength that God can give us ... You ask, what is our aim? I can answer in one word: Victory ... at all costs, victory in spite of all terror, victory however long and hard the road may be: for without victory there can be no survival.
>
> We shall go on to the end. We shall fight in France. We shall fight on the seas and the oceans. We shall fight with growing confidence and growing strength in the air. We shall defend our island, whatever the cost may be; we shall fight on the beaches, we shall fight on the landing grounds, we shall fight in the fields and in the streets, we shall fight in the hills; we shall never surrender.

VISION CREATES CHALLENGE

In the 1930s, the General Electric Company supposedly had a practical joke that it played on every new engineer in its incandescent lighting group. Each new engineer began by meeting with the director of the division. The director would turn on an incandescent light bulb and observe, 'Do you see the hot spot in this bulb?' (In those days you could almost see the filament even though the bulb had a coating on it.) 'Your job is to develop a new coating that smoothes that illumination out so that the entire surface of the bulb glows in a uniform manner.'

With the assignment clear, the young engineer would go off to tackle this problem. What the rest of the firm knew, was that it could not be done. After several weeks of struggle the new engineer would admit defeat and then, to the immense amusement of his colleagues who had also failed, he would be enlightened about the impossibility of his task.

And it was a good joke as an initiation rite until around 1952 when a newly hired engineer returned to the director, screwed his bulb into the socket, and turned it on. 'Is this what you were looking for, Sir?' he asked. And, as the director looked at the first bulb that met his impossible conditions, he is reported to have said, 'Ah, yup! That's it!'

The initiation ruse was dead. The joke was over. But a new way to coat the inside of light bulbs had been discovered. The vision had become reality.

VISION SEES THE INVISIBLE

Walter went out to the country with his friend. They drove off the main road through a grove of orange trees to a mostly uninhabited piece of land, just a few horses grazing amongst a couple of old tumble-down shacks. Walter stopped the car and began to describe vividly what he was going to build on that site. He very much wanted his friend Arthur to buy some of the land surrounding his project. Walter explained, 'I can handle the main project myself. It will take all the money I can raise, but ... I want you to have the first option on purchasing the surrounding acreage because in the next five years it will increase in value many hundreds of times.'

Arthur thought to himself, 'Who in the world is going to drive twenty-five miles out of town for a crazy project like that? Walter's dream must have caused him to lose sight of reality. He's out of his mind!' Arthur excused himself with delaying tactics and mumbled something about considering it later when his bank account was looking better. 'Later on will be too late,' Walter cautioned. 'You'd better move on it right now.' But Arthur failed to act.

Little did Art Linklater realise that he was turning down the opportunity to buy unlimited acreage alongside what was soon to become Disneyland. Had he done what his good friend Walt Disney had urged him to do, he would have made himself a fortune!

Walt Disney died before the vast Disneyland project was completed. His wife was asked to open it on his behalf. A sympathiser beside her remarked how sad it was that Disney had never lived to see all this! She silenced him with an immediate response, 'Oh but he did!'

VISION MEANS THERE IS SOMETHING TO AIM AT

Playing golf on Turnberry in Scotland a few years ago, an old Scotsman who had been caddying for years gave Ken Blanchard a significant tip. After Ken had hit a big drive that ended up in the deep rough off the fairway, the caddy commented in a brogue beloved by North Americans, 'Laddie, when you hit your driving club aim for a specific spot on the fairway. If you miss that spot, you will probably still be on the fairway, but if you just aim for the fairway, and miss that you will be where we are [now] laddie – in big trouble.' (Ken Blanchard and Don Shula, *The Little Book of Coaching*)

EVEN NEWCOMERS GET VISIONS

J. A. Baker was lecturing at a famous research facility on the valuable role of people in industry on the fringes of power. During the break a young woman came up to him and said, 'You need to say one more thing about outsiders. We are very fragile and break easily.'

Baker continues the story:

'I agreed that it was a good point. Then I observed, "You said 'we'. What happened to you?" She shared the following story:

She had joined her company three years before. About a month later she had a 'big' idea.

'How big?' I asked.

'Worth about five hundred million dollars,' she answered!

She was very excited about the idea so she put together her notes and called the director. She said she would like to talk to him and he replied by telling her to come on up, because he 'loved talking to his new people'.

She said the first couple of minutes was friendly chitchat, getting-to-know-you kind of talk. Then, when there came the inevitable lull, she pulled out her notes and began presenting her idea.

She said that as she talked, the director became more and more agitated. After just a couple more minutes, he stood up from behind his desk, walked around it, picked up her notes, took her by the arm, and began escorting her to the door.

As they reached it he said, 'Had you been working here for five years I might have heard you out.' With that, he sent her on her way.

I commiserated with her. Then I asked what had happened to her idea. She said that a competitor had just announced a product that looked very like her idea.

'Ouch,' I said.

Then she made her closing comment and walked away. I will never forget what she had to say:

'I've since had six ideas better than that one . . . but I haven't been here five years yet.'[10]

VISIONARIES SEE WHAT OTHERS CAN'T SEE

The late J. Paul Getty, once thought to be the richest man in the world, made most of his fortune from oil. Early in his career, he owned just one a small piece of property, 72-foot square, in the Seal Beach oil field of California. Oil derricks of the day needed plenty of room and it seemed he was stymied with too little space to bring in the necessary equipment. The oilmen around referred to his little plot as 'Getty's turnip patch'!

But Getty was sure there must be some way by which he could extract the oil beneath his plot and was determined to find a way to drill a well there. He asked a drilling crew for suggestions. They came up with the idea of building a miniature oil derrick to fit on his tiny 'patch'. The narrow path connecting the road to the site made access for the equipment seem impossible. But they built a miniature railroad track along this narrow strip to carry a miniature derrick to the site. And the well they drilled produced thousands of barrels of oil over a period of many years.

During his lifetime Getty proved, time and again, that organisational problems can be solved if leaders are willing to solicit creative ideas from other people and then see that they are put into practice.

PRAYER

Lord, you have said, 'Blessed are the pure in heart for they shall see you.' Grant me such guarding of my eyes to keep them clear; such honest confession of my sins to keep me clean, and such humbling of my heart to keep it open. Give me the grace to discern a true vision from you or to whomsoever you may choose to grant it. Then help me with insight to understand the conviction to commmmmunicate it, and the wisdom to implement it, for the sake of your kingdom and glory. Amen.

'Show me thy ways, O LORD; teach me thy paths' (Psalm 25:4 KJV).

CHAPTER 4

People who seek
after holiness

*'And a highway shall be there ... And it shall be called the **Highway
of Holiness**. The unclean shall not pass over it, ...
But the redeemed shall walk there.'*
(ISAIAH 35:8,9 NKJV, EMPHASIS ADDED).

'Follow after holiness without which no man shall see the Lord'.
(HEBREWS 12:14)

'It is God's will that you should be sanctified.'
(1 THESSALONIANS 4:3 NIV)

We hear too little preaching today and have too few articles and
popular books on holiness. Perhaps the changes required to be holy
are too challenging, or mistaken teaching of the past has put us off.
We have seen how some of this teaching has turned into unfortunate
parodies such as:

Pharisaism – 'I thank God I am not as other men are' – self-
righteous, legalistic, judgemental, joyless, puritanical and
unforgiving practitioners.
Christian perfectionism – super-spiritual, sanctimonious, intensive,
over scrupulous, exclusive, sectarian and phoney practitioners.
Gnosticism – A mistaken belief that all spirit is good and all matter
is evil, leading to mistaken views of sex, etc and a retreat from social
issues.

Because of one or other of these misrepresentations, talk of the *holy*
went sour on the church. Nevertheless as it must be an essential

ingredient in the believer's soul, so it must be disentangled from that false teaching and fake representation associated with it in the mind of so many Christians.

The worst possible scenario is for church members not to be growing more Christ-like, which is, after all, what holiness is all about. For this we will find that Christ gives us his grace. Martin Luther has observed that, 'The real and true work of the passion of Christ is to conform us to Christ.' There is not much new to be said about holiness. It is the unique characteristic of our God. 'Holy, holy, holy, is the Lord of Hosts'. This has been true from the beginning, is true now and will be true for evermore. God may change his attitude but he will never change his nature. He is just utterly HOLY. St Peter reminds us that God wants his children to be like him. 'As he who called you is *holy*, be *holy* yourselves in all your conduct, for it is written, "You shall be *holy*, for I am *holy*."' (1 Peter 1:15,16 NRSV, emphasis added).

So the first obligation of any leader is to be holy. The Scottish saint and church leader, Murray McCheyne, summed this up aptly when he wrote, 'My people's greatest need is my own personal holiness.' Obviously saintliness does not make a leader, but no one should aspire to lead God's people, who does not aspire after holiness.

All church leaders have the responsibility of guiding their people into the ways of holiness. They do this through their example: 'Make every effort to live in peace with all men and to *be holy; without holiness no-one will see the Lord*' (Hebrews 12:14 NIV, emphasis added).

CHRIST SHOWS THE WAY

Jesus Christ, the Holy Son of God, in whom dwells all the fulness of the Godhead bodily (Colossians 2:9), is the unique earthly model of holiness for us.

One way in which his holy character clearly developed was through his disciplined prayer life. The Gospels draw frequent attention to Jesus' habit of prayer. Indeed the disciples begged Jesus to teach them how to pray too (Luke 11:1–13). Good prayer communication was obviously vital to Jesus in his relationship with his Father.

FRUIT OF THE SPIRIT LEADS TO HOLINESS

Then there is the crucifying of the flesh (Paul says, 'I die daily') and the cultivating of the fruit of the Spirit (Galatians 5:22,23), 'fruit' of love, joy, peace, longsuffering, kindness, goodness, faithfulness, gentleness, and self-control. All this is elemental to genuine seekers after holiness.

UNCLEANNESS AND IMPURITY MIRE THE LIFE OF HOLINESS

'Blessed are the pure in heart for they shall see God' (Matthew 5:8). If part of the unique nature of God is his holiness, so the perverse nature of Satan is unholy and is characterised by uncleanness and immorality. Babylon, in the Bible, is symbolic of Satan's domain, and the originator of every system opposed to God. It is depicted in the Bible as the mother of harlots with whom the kings of the earth committed fornication.

Probably one of the most constant assaults on a leader's striving after holiness is the temptation to sexual impurity. This problem is no new tactic of the enemy. Sigmund Freud thought that the power of sexuality was the strongest force we have to deal with in life and the novelist Frederick Buechner described it as 'the ape that gibbers in my loins'.

The book of Proverbs in the Bible warns against the adulterous woman who stands at the street corner enticing men, 'Many are the victims she has brought down, many mighty men are among her slain' (7:26). St Bernard of Clairvaux, a 12th-century abbot, once remarked, 'To be always with a woman and not to have intercourse with her is more difficult than to raise the dead.' Sexual temptation is sometimes blatantly obvious but can often be quite subtle. Bud Palmer warns, 'For most of us in the local church ministry, sexual temptation doesn't come painted in lurid tones. It comes in the quieter, gentle relationships that a pastor has with the people he truly loves.'

William Coe, 1693–1729,[1] a regular church layman who thanks God for survival in accidents on horseback, for his wife's deliverance in childbearing, repents for sleeping in church during the service and being slightly dishonest in business dealings, records in his diary in 1718 that he repents because

'I have often pleased my selfe [sic] with impure fanicyes [sic] and thoughts and ... [deleted] And in unchaste songs and filthy and unclean talking – I have often resolved against my mispending pretious tyme, [sic] yet ...

An Episcopalian friend of mine in California fell in love with a woman he was counselling, and left his faithful wife and family to marry her. Truly 'the heart is deceitful ... and desperately wicked' (Jeremiah 17:9 KJV), and that includes all of us. We may be new creatures in Christ but we still get deceived and defeated by our old nature, and we soon find, like St Paul, that this 'old nature – the flesh' has to be kept under control and mortified daily as we work out our salvation with fear and trembling. From Philip Barker we read, 'The fire of passion should not, and cannot, be extinguished, but it must be controlled and sexually channelled.'

Some teachers have thought that Romans chapter 7 must have been Paul's experience before his conversion. But most of us, if we are honest, resonate with his lament, 'O wretched man that I am! who shall deliver me from the body of this death?'(v 24 KJV) This is also our lament about thed nature still within us. But the chapter ends with hope, 'I thank God through Jesus Christ ...' (v 25).

That's the good news for those who really want to be holy. The Spirit of God is on our side and is working with us and in us as we strive after holiness. 'And we, who with unveiled faces all reflect the Lord's glory, are being transformed into his likeness with ever-increasing glory, which comes from the Lord, who is the Spirit' (2 Corinthians 3:18 NIV). One of the major ways the Spirit does this is through the Word he inspired, the Bible. Peter writes, 'Like new born babies, crave pure spiritual milk, so that by it you may grow up in your salvation, ... grow in the grace and knowledge of ... Jesus Christ' (1 Peter 2:2; 2 Peter 3:18 NIV).

SEXUAL PURITY IN THE LIFE OF HOLINESS

In his delightful book, *Pleasures for Evermore*, Sam Storms writes a chapter on 'Sex and Integrity' where he reminds his readers that sex was originally God's idea. 'God created us as sexual beings and no one wants our sexual satisfaction more than God.' Yet the battles in the area of sex can be unrelenting and powerful. I once heard it said that the average American male had a sexual fantasy every twelve minutes.

Philip Barker adds, 'The power of sex can dismantle our life faster and with more fury than anything else. When it is unleashed it seems that normal, rational human beings will sacrifice anything to its insistence.' There, but for the grace of God, go most of us!

Storms was actually writing his chapter on the subject of sex at the time of President Bill Clinton's unprecedented testimony before a grand jury in which he 'confessed' to having misled his family and the American people about his relationship with a 21-year-old intern in the White House. Storms continues,

> As if that was not bad enough, one needed only to wait until today [18 August 1998], to hear the reactions of people around the nation. Amazingly, the majority of those interviewed by the media didn't seem to care that our (married) president had engaged in sexual activity with a young lady not much older than his own daughter. They were even less concerned that he had lied about it to everyone on national TV.

Would it be any different in Britain? Surely we live among an equally crooked and perverse generation! But the kingdom of God is totally different; it is built on righteousness. One way this is expressed is through holiness of living in our relationship with God and with everyone else, including our spouses and families. How a man relates to his wife will have a direct effect on his relationship to Christ and will also significantly impact his work. Sam Storms goes on to say that 'at the heart of purity is purity of heart' and the heart of purity is sexual purity and integrity.

GOD'S WILL IS FOR HOLINESS

Paul presses the point when he writes, 'This is the will of God, your sanctification: that you should abstain from sexual immorality; that each of you should know how to possess his own vessel in sanctification and honour, not in passion of lust, like the Gentiles who do not know God' (1 Thessalonians 4:3 NKJV).

Thankfully, with every temptation God promises a way of escape if we want it (1 Corinthians 10:13). How often leaders will need to do what Joseph did when Potiphar's wife tried to seduce him. He simply fled from the scene (Genesis 39:12). Paul passed on the same advice to Timothy, 'Flee … youthful lusts' (2 Timothy 2:22 KJV).

SELF-CONTROL FOR HOLINESS

This, of course, is one of the gifts of the Spirit we are to cultivate, and we often need some practical help. Healthy disciplines help us to avoid the devil's wiles. He still finds plenty of evil work for idle hands, and carnal thoughts for empty minds.

David Seamands tells an amusing story of an old alchemist who used to sell the locals a powder which he claimed would turn water into gold, 'But when you mix it,' he said, 'you must never think of red monkeys, or it will not work.' So no one ever got the gold because no one could ever force themselves not to think of those red monkeys.

You cannot force yourself not to think of something – the only thing is to think of something different, and as St Paul reminds us, we need to focus our thinking on higher things: '… whatever is true, whatever is noble, whatever is right, whatever is pure, whatever is lovely, whatever is admirable … think about such things' (Philippians 4:8 NIV).

SELF-GIVING LOVE

If there was one thing that drew people to follow the Holy Son of God it was his self-effacement and self-giving. He was moved with compassion on many occasions. He went out of his way to serve people in need – lepers, prostitutes, widows, children, the sick, the lame, the halt and the blind – people who could do nothing for him in return. It seemed of no benefit to him if he helped them; it was just that he saw they had a need that he knew he could meet. His motivation was purely altruistic. He was never self-seeking nor self-serving.

A person with those attributes is so like God, who has been defined by Otto Piper as 'Wholly Other'. Such followers are soon noticed in the community for their 'wholly other-ness', so Christ-like, so different from the ordinary run of men and women in the community.

A PRACTICAL SPUR TO BE HOLY

I once picked up a Christian magazine in the United States and jotted down a list of specific consequences, which pastor Randy

Alcorn had written down to help leaders as they faced sexual temptations. He spelt out some of the consequences that could follow as a reminder to himself whenever he felt himself vulnerable to sexual immorality. I have slightly amended his list:

- Grieving the Lord who redeemed me
- Dragging the Lord's sacred name into the mud
- Facing a Righteous Judge on the Last Day, to give an account of my actions
- Following in the footsteps of these people (List names – TV evangelists) whose immorality forfeited their ministries and caused me to shudder
- Inflicting untold hurt on (name) my best friend and my loyal wife
- Losing my wife's respect and trust
- Hurting my beloved sons, (List names), and daughters, (List names), their loved ones, and my grandchildren, and losing their respect and trust
- Destroying my example and credibility with my children, and nullifying both the present and future efforts to teach them to obey God. (My child will think, 'Why listen to a man who betrayed both my mother and us?')
- Causing shame to my family. ('Why isn't Daddy a minister in the church any more?')
- Losing my self-respect
- Creating a form of guilt awfully hard to shake off. Even though God were to forgive me would I ever be able to forgive myself?
- Forming memories and flashbacks that could plague my future intimacy with my wife
- Wasting years of ministry training and experience for a long time, maybe permanently
- Forfeiting the effect of years of witnessing to my parents and in-laws and reinforcing their distrust of ministers, which has begun to soften by my example, but which would harden, perhaps permanently, because of my immorality
- Undermining the faithful example and hard work of other Christians in our community

- Bringing great pleasure to Satan, the enemy of God and all that is good
- Heaping judgement and endless difficulty on the person with whom I committed adultery
- Bearing physical consequences, possibly of such diseases as gonorrhoea, syphilis, chlamydia, herpes and AIDS – perhaps infecting my wife, or in the case of AIDS, even causing her death. Or that of my child.
- Possibly causing a pregnancy, with personal and financial implications, including a life-long reminder of my sin
- Depriving my illegitimate offspring of the normal rights by my not being there for him or her
- Bringing shame and hurt to these fellow ministers and church leaders (List names)
- Causing shame and hurt to these friends, especially those whom I have led personally to Christ and discipled (List names)
- Invoking shame and life-long embarrassment upon myself.

QUOTES

- God's holy people require holy leadership. (David Pytches)
- To walk with God means keeping a good relationship – Adam didn't. He was alienated. Enoch did. He was translated. (David Pytches)
- The true Christian ideal is not to be happy but to be holy. (A. W. Tozer)
- Holiness is not a condition into which we drift. (John Stott)
- Lord give me chastity, but not yet. (St. Augustine of Hippo, as a young man)
- The Christian leader is called by God. He is a person of Christ-like character. He possesses functional competence. (George Barna)
- Leaders must be walking the walk before they begin talking the talk. (Bill Hybels)
- Wel oghte a prest ensample for to yive, By his clennesse, how that his sheep shold live. (Chaucer's Prologue for *Canterbury Tales*)
- The average so-called Bible Christian in our times is but a wretched parody of true Sainthood. (A. W. Tozer)
- *My Utmost for His Highest*. (Oswald Chambers)

- What a kennel of hell-hounds we find hidden in the human heart. (Alexander White)
- He that sees the beauty of holiness, or true moral good, sees the greatest and most important thing in the world. (Jonathan Edwards)
- There is no true holiness without humility. (Thomas Fuller)
- In our era the road to holiness necessarily passes through the world of action. (Dag Hammarskjold)
- Holiness is the habit of being of one mind with God.[2] (J. C. Ryle)
- We must be holy because this is the one reason why Christ came into the world. (J. C. Ryle)
- We must be holy because this is the only proof that we love the Lord Jesus with sincerity. (J. C. Ryle)
- Growing in holiness is like riding a bike. If you stop pedalling, you fall off. (Rob Warner)

ILLUSTRATIONS
What the prophet saw

In a remarkable vision, Isaiah saw the Lord sitting on a throne high and lifted up, and the seraphim around the throne were crying, '*Holy, holy, holy* is the LORD of hosts; the whole earth is full of His glory!' ... And he (Isaiah) said, 'Woe is me, for I am undone! Because I am a man of unclean lips And I dwell in the midst of a people of unclean lips, For my eyes have seen the King, the LORD of Hosts' (Isaiah 6: 3,5 NKJV, emphasis added).

Total commitment

I will tell you the secret (of my life). God has had all that there was of me. There have been men with greater brains than I had, men with greater opportunities. But I made up my mind that God should have all of William Booth that there was. (General William Booth was the founder of the Salvation Army)

Other worldly

Lancelot Andrews (1555–1626), author of a private devotional called *Preces Privatae*, was both Royal Almoner and Bishop of Chichester. He was a familiar court figure on all state occasions, who 'never quite belonged to his own crooked and perverse generation'.

He spent hours in prayer. 'He seemed to be clothed in a garment of sanctity amid a society so hollow and petty and vicious. His charity and kindliness in human relations made men at once ashamed and thankful.' (Florence Higham)

God's hour

The late US Cardinal Archbishop Joseph Benadin gave an interview with *Newsweek* (23 November 1996) in which he shared his personal testimony about his own private prayer life:

> I learned many years ago that the only way I could give quality time to prayer was by getting up early in the morning. (I must add parenthetically that I didn't have a great desire to get up so early – I usually tried to stay in bed as late as I could). In the early hours of the morning before the phones and the doorbells started to ring, before the mail arrived, seemed to me to be the best for giving quality time to the Lord. So I promised God and myself that I would give the first hour of each day to prayer. This does not mean that I have learned to pray perfectly. It doesn't mean that I have not experienced the struggles that other people have faced. Quite the contrary! But early on, I made another decision. I said, 'Lord, I know that I spend a certain amount of that morning hour of prayer day-dreaming, problem-solving, and I'm not sure that I can cut that out. I'll try, but the important thing is, I am not going to give that time to anybody else. So even though it may not connect me as much with you as it should, nobody else is going to get that time.

Give me your mornings

Martin Down relates how impressed he was by the way God had once spoken to John Arnott, the leading pastor in the then Airport Vineyard, where the Toronto blessing was being poured out in the 1990s . This was soon impacting leaders from all over the world. Arnott shared with some leaders how, a few months before the blessing fell in Toronto, God had said to him, 'John, give me your mornings'!

Martin Down had a disciplined prayer life that he had sought to maintain faithfully, but 'those words turned my understanding, not just of my prayers, but of my whole life on its head. Up till then I had supposed it was for my own benefit that I prayed. All of a sudden I saw that God wanted me to spend time with him to please him.'

The heart of purity is purity of the heart

As a teenager shopping in Ipswich I would occasionally see nuns in their black habits walking the streets in pairs. I did not know much about the 'religious' life in those days. It all seemed rather strange to me but whenever two nuns passed by they always lowered their gaze as they approached the opposite sex. Under their vows of chastity they were no doubt seeking to avoid the possible temptation of sensual desire. This discipline may have seemed extreme but their hearts were so right. A major element of holiness is purity and that certainly involves sexual purity. Those holy nuns were following the example of Job who said so long ago, 'I have made a covenant with my eyes; Why then should I look upon a young woman?' (Job 31:1 NKJV)

What kind of example?

For my own confirmation (aged 14) my father gave me a Bible in which he had inscribed, in his own hand, words that I have never forgotten, words from the Apostle Paul counselling the younger leader Timothy, 'Let no one despise your youth, but be an example to the believers in word, in conduct, in love, in spirit, in faith, *in purity*' (1 Timothy 4:12 NKJV, emphasis added).

EXHORTATION

'Dear friends, I urge you, as aliens and strangers in the world, to abstain from sinful desires, which war against your soul. Live such good lives among the pagans that, though they accuse you of doing wrong, they may see your good deeds and glorify God on the day he visits us' (1 Peter 2:11,12 NIV).

HYMN

Oh, to be saved from myself, dear Lord,
Oh, to be lost in Thee,
Oh, that it might be no more I,
But Christ that lives in me.

PRAYERS

Lord, lead us not into temptation but deliver us from evil! Amen.

'Search me, O God, and know my heart:
try me, and know my thoughts:
And see if there be any wicked way in me,
and lead me in the way everlasting' (Psalm 139:23,24 KJV).

Lord you have called us to be a kingdom of priests and a holy nation.
We confess that we have fallen far short of what you expect and what
we would want to be. Once again we ask for your pardon and
forgiveness through the cross of Calvary. Sanctify and renew us
through the inspiration of your Holy Spirit. Grant to us the grace to
develop self-control, through Jesus Christ our Lord. Amen.

CHAPTER 5

People with inquisitive minds

'Love the Lord thy God with all … thy mind.'
(MATTHEW 22:37 KJV)

'The honour of kings is to search out a matter.'
(PROVERBS 25:2 KJV)

'Who is this who darkens counsel by words without knowledge?'
(JOB 38:2 NKJV)

'Be not wise in your own conceits.'
(ROMANS 12:16 KJV)

An ignorant layman is an embarrassment;
an ignorant priest is a scandal.
(DAILY TELEGRAPH 4 MARCH 2004)

I wish he had approached the problem with an open mind
rather than an open mouth.
(ONE AMERICAN SENATOR OF ANOTHER)

The important thing is not to stop questioning -
never to lose holy curiosity.
(ALBERT EINSTEIN)

Cleric comes from the ecclesiastical Latin 'clericus' meaning
'a learned person'.

Our mission 'is not just to win souls but to save minds.
If you win the whole world and … [lose its mind] … you will discover
that you have not won the world.

Indeed it may turn out that you have actually lost it.'
(CHARLES MALIK)

*Evangelicals cannot afford to go on living on the periphery of
responsible intellectual existence.*[1]
(MARK NOLL)

A holy curiosity

It would be tragic if all our efforts at grooming practitioners left the
future church in the grip of non-reflective anti-intellectuals. Our
ministry is to the mind as well as the body and soul. We need to be
acquiring facts to inform the mind. John Locke, the English
philosopher, once wrote of how he came to be regarded as
intellectual:

> I attribute the little I know to my not having been ashamed to
> ask for information and to ... conversing with all descriptions
> of men on those topics that formed their own peculiar
> professions and pursuits.

Another obvious way to enlarge the mind is the regular reading of
good books. A recent survey revealed that clergy spend less time
reading books than accountants, chefs, secretaries and taxi drivers. If
this is so, they must not be surprised if laymen pay them little respect
and attention. God is ever renewing the minds of Christians by his
Spirit. Leaders then should replenish their renewed minds constantly,
and always have an uplifting book on the go. Leaders need to pause
often, reflect on what they have discovered and find every way
possible to use it for illustrating God's truth.

Billy Graham used to urge his audiences to read the newspaper
every day and keep abreast of what was going in the world. So many
faithful preachers can be really boring because they are so
uninteresting. Interesting people are interesting because they do
interesting things, see interesting plays and films, meet interesting
people, and read interesting books.

A leader does not have to be an intellectual genius but should be
an inquisitive sort of person. Leaders should be happy to confront
complex and abstract problems. While some Christian leaders may
not consider themselves intellectuals they may have a higher IQ than

they realise. They may not have achieved high grades at school but still have a high intelligence. I was intrigued, when working among the Araucanian Indians in central Chile, to find that although so many men and women I met had had a poor education, so many showed great intelligence. And some people who have had serious learning disabilities in their childhood or had lacked motivation in their home environment have often proved themselves to be quite remarkable late learners. Twenty-year-old Hitomi Kanchara the recent winner of Japan's top literary award with her novel *Snakes and Earings* was a grammar schol drop out.

LATERAL THINKING

Some of us have discovered ourselves to be lateral thinkers (a term invented and popularised by Edward de Bono), which may explain the reason we have experienced so much diversion and loss of mental focus even in a privileged learning environment. The lateral thinker can easily get caught up in pondering side issues arising from a speaker's address, and frequently lose the main thrust of a linear argument. But lateral thinkers are able to contribute many creative insights because they look at problems or situations from a different perspective.

LEADERS SHOULD REFLECT ON THE PAST, THE PRESENT AND THE FUTURE

The past:

We must disagree with Henry Ford when he said 'History is bunk'. We believe that history is relevant to the whole of life. Alexandr Solzhenitsyn believes that 'A people that no longer remembers has lost its history and its soul.' At a moment of particular frustration in the 1920s, Winston Churchill wrote to a friend about the importance of understanding the past:

> How strange it is that the past is so little understood and so quickly forgotten. We live in the most thoughtless of ages. Every day headlines and short reviews. I have tried to drag history up a little nearer to our own times in case it should be a help as a guide in present difficulties.

Churchill has written several volumes of history including a four volume *History of the English Speaking People*, so his letter reflects a real appreciation of subject. It was his grasp of history that prepared him for leadership in World War II.

It's a cliché, but history does tend to repeat itself. What goes round comes round! Churchill reckoned that if only Hitler had studied European history better he would never have started World War II. He would have known he was going to lose it. There are good lessons to be learned from the past. As Konrad Adenauer has put it, 'History is the sum total of things that could have been avoided.'

But again, the things that could have been avoided are not the sum total of history, and since history has created our traditions, when we advocate change we should be careful not to underestimate the values of the past. Many people, especially church members, find their spirituality intrinsically bound up with their traditions; history in fact has shaped their souls. So if we scorn the lessons of the past we may alienate the very folk we need to help us in building for the future. We don't have to let the past be a burden. But neither do we need to repudiate it: we respect it so that we can learn from it.

The present

Our world is the reality we live in, the here and now, the present. It is a world crying out for God's compassion and mercy. One of the dangers of church is that members can become progressively cut off from the world around them and have no 'friends among the mammon of unrighteousness'. The church is called to be salt, light and leaven *in the world*. We have all heard of those who are so heavenly minded that they are no earthly use. There are still plenty who are just like that. Let's be well informed about what is going on in the wider world and involved with the needs, cultures and challenges in our local community. 'Think globally: act locally' is a 'green' slogan, which has beneficial applications for all of us. There are always new opportunities for new enterprises around us.

Alan Jamieson, a Christian sociologist, in discussing reasons why people leave their churches today, observes that members feel stifled by small mindedness and inhibited by petty shibboleths. They feel frustrated by their church environment when it is so cut off and exclusive. In his book, *A Churchless Faith*, he describes them as 'personally faith limiting churches'.

There is a church in Ealing that advertises itself as 'A Church for the Community' and has exciting engagement with the people around them, which is very beneficial, both to the community and to the church itself.

The Future

The future is rushing towards us at breakneck speed. Our vision must be for the future. Charles Kettering has said, 'I spend most of my life thinking about the future because that's where I am going to spend the rest of my life.' A concept of the future must involve all our decision-making.

Theresa May, Chairperson of the Tory Party, remarked in Blackpool in October 2003 that, 'We are building for the future. There's no future in the past.'

We can draw lessons from the past but we cannot live by it. '... do not dwell on the past. See, I am doing a new thing! ... do you not perceive it?' (Isaiah 43:18,19 NIV). Leaders of secular organisations, more than any others, are continually reflecting and reckoning with the future; it is a constant preoccupation, an instinctive exercise in foresight. Manufacturers don't want to be making things for which materials will not be available, for markets that will no longer exist, nor for prices with which they cannot compete.

QUOTES

- Leaders are readers. (Anon)
- Today a reader. Tomorrow a leader. (W. Fusselman)
- Incompleteness is at the heart of all knowledge. (Anon)
- Our God is bigger than our boxes. (Andrew Blyth)
- Leaders value the creative role of lateral thinkers. (de Bono)
- Leaders understand the varied but essential elements of a creative team. (Anon)
- A leader has to surround himself with a complementary staff. (Rudolph Giuliani)
- The value of his college education was summarised by a grateful student who wrote later to his esteemed headmaster, 'You showed me where North is'! (Anon)
- One's destination is never a place but rather a new way of looking at things. (Henry Miller)
- Education is not the filling of a pail. It is the lighting of a fire. (Anon)

- I don't by any means think that a grasshopper mind is a great disability for a newspaper editor. (Max Hastings, one-time editor of the *Daily Telegraph*)
- Theology has the mission of seeking out answers to new and urgent problems. The deposit of faith is not a stagnant cistern. It is a Spring of Living Waters' (L. Boff)
- Intellect is not a head ready stored with knowledge but a feel for discovering data when it is wanted, and what is relevant for resolving the problems in hand. (Anon)
- Knowledge is the raw material out of which the finest of all machines, the mind, creates its amazing world. (A. W. Tozer)
- The rate of change today requires that each of us becomes a frantic learner. (Max De Pree)
- Study the past if you would divine the future. (Confucious)
- Leaders, like Moses, must be men of far horizons. (Anon)
- Responsible leadership is always leaning into the future, watching how our policies affect not only the practices of the present but the people of tomorrow. (Anon)
- Leaders are accountable for the continuous renewal of the organisation. (Max De Pree)
- New Wine Skins are made up of the same elements as the Old Wine Skins – except for the fizz. (David Pytches)
- If you read history you will find that the Christians who did most for the present world were precisely those who thought most of the next. (C. S. Lewis)
- Renewal requires that leaders be alive in a special way to innovation and be hospitable to the creative person. (Max DePree)
- Leaders today need to have a global outlook ... the fact is no one has a monopoly of good ideas, and no one country or organisation has a monopoly on good people. (Sven-Goran Eriksson)
- Quite often, when a man thinks his mind is getting broader, it's only his conscience stretching.
- Our past may have created us but it must not control us. (Anon)
- Your life is shaped by the end you live for. You are made in the image of what you desire. (Thomas Merton)

- The man who never alters his opinion is like standing water, and breeds reptiles of the mind. (William Blake)
- Very few people take the trouble to use their brains as long as their prejudices are in working condition. (Roy Smith)
- The important thing is not to stop questioning ... never lose a holy curiosity. (Albert Einstein)
- I attribute the little I know to my not having been ashamed to ask for information and to my... conversing with all descriptions of men on those topics that form their own peculiar professions and pursuits. (John Locke, English philosopher)
- I am defeated, and know it, if I meet any human being from whom I find myself unable to learn anything. (George Herbert Palmer)
- Those who do not know history are forever condemned to repeat it. (Will Durant)
- A page of history is worth a volume of logic. (Oliver Wendell Holmes)
- The history of the world is the judge of the world. (Herman Ullmann)
- Dear Friend, never denigrate truth! Never disdain theology! Never despise your mind! If you do you grieve the Holy Spirit of Truth. (John Stott)
- Evangelicals need to repent of their refusal to think Christianly and to develop the mind of Christ. (Os Guinness)

ILLUSTRATIONS
Expanding horizons
In a book by an expert on mentoring, *Mentors and Protégés*, the author spells out one of her objectives for those who seek her help: 'to expand their horizons and perspectives' and 'improve their ... intellectual development'. (Linda Phillips-Jones)

Still learning
Somewhere deep down I think I must have had the notion that once I had learned the ropes of being a vicar (perhaps after two or three years), I could easily settle into the job and take it in my stride. Here I am eighteen years later, *feeling as much a learner as I have ever done*.

(Robert Warren) (italics added)

Paying the price

It costs so much to be a full human being, that there are very few who have the enlightenment or the courage to pay the price. One has to abandon altogether the search for security and reach out to the risk of living with both arms outstretched. One has to embrace the world like a lover. One has to accept pain as a condition of existence. One has to court doubt and darkness as the cost of knowing. One needs a will that is stubborn in conflict, but studious of all the consequence of living and dying. (Anon)

Ignorance causes trouble

A Chinaman and a Jew got into a brawl. Something about the Oriental had infuriated the Jew who punched him shouting, 'That's for Pearl Harbour!'

'Pearl Harbour? I'm Chinese,' responded the Oriental plaintively. 'It was the Japanese who attacked Pearl Harbour.'

'Japanese, Chinese,' snorted the Jew, 'they are all the same to me.'

The Chinaman then struck back at the Jew. 'That's for the Titanic.'

'Titanic!' muttered the Jew. 'The Titanic was sunk by an iceberg!'

The Oriental shrugged his shoulders, 'Iceberg, Goldberg, Steinberg, they're all the same to me. (Adapted from *The Devil's Dictionary* 1906)

Asking the right questions

According to William Hague, George W. Bush is 'far, far brighter than his reputation. 'When my friend Richard Perle, now one of his leading defence policy advisors, first went along to brief Candidate Bush with all the military experts and endless charts and tables, Mr Bush stopped them as they were about to make their presentation. "Now, I know you are about to show me a lot of figures," he said. "First of all I want to discuss what the American Armed Forces are for and what our objectives are and then the figures will fall into place."

'Perle and his colleagues were enormously impressed, not by Mr Bush's knowledge at that stage, but by his readiness to admit to what he did not know, and his ability to ask the right questions. He avoids getting mired in detail without thinking things up from first principles, and as a result is able to think "out of the box".[3] (William Hague)

Trying to understand

I know you believe you understand
What you think I said
But I am not sure you realise
That what you heard is not what I meant. (Anon)

Seeing ahead

He had a quick brain, and could visualise things ahead, and as far as he could, he safeguarded any eventuality that was likely to occur. (Lionel Greenstreet, First officer of the *Endurance*, writing of Sir Ernest Shackleton, the Antarctic explorer)

Seeing beneath the surface

Perception of ideas rather than the storing of them, should be the aim of education. The mind should be an eye to see rather than a bin to store facts in. The man who has been taught by the Holy Spirit will be a seer rather than a scholar. The difference is that the scholar sees, and the seer sees through. (A. W. Tozer)

Dangers of anti-intellectualism

The arena of creative thinking is abdicated and vacated to the enemy … Who among the evangelical scholars is quoted as a normative source by the greatest secular authorities on history or philosophy or psychology or sociology or politics. Does your mode of thinking have the slightest chance of becoming the dominant mode of thinking in the great universities of Europe and America, which stamp your entire civilisation with their own spirit and ideas? (Mark Noll)

Prayers

Lord, deliver us from pettiness. Give us both revelations of your will and sanctify our common sense in working through our everyday affairs. Create in us the space for breadth and balance to understand the arguments of others and to comprehend what is behind them, even when their logic seems weak or their emotionalism off-putting.

Keep us ever fresh in our relationship with you who never quenched a smoking flax. Help us ever to rejoice in the wonder of your works and the mystery of your ways, which are past finding out. Amen.

Lord in your Everlasting Kingdom time is swallowed up into eternity. But whilst we still live in Time help us not to be ignorant of the Past, nor uncaring of the Present, nor unconcerned about the Future. Help us fully to fulfil our responsibilities in this life so that we might be found faithful in the next. Amen.

Lord Jesus Christ, you have called us to be your disciples,
Deliver us from the pride of thinking
we have learned all we need to know,
done all we need to do
and become all we need to be.
As we remember that disciples are learners
enable us continually to learn as we follow you
for your name's sake. Amen.
(Maurice Burrell)

CHAPTER 6

People who value wisdom

Get wisdom; get insight

(PROVERBS 4:4)

*'Jesus increased in wisdom and stature, and in favour
with God and man.'*

(LUKE 2:52 KJV)

*'And the Child grew and became strong in spirit, filled with wisdom;
and the grace of God was upon Him.'*

(LUKE 2:40 NKJV)

*'All who heard Him [the 12-year-old Jesus] were astonished at His
understanding and answers.'*

(LUKE 2:47 NKJV)

*'... they were astonished and said "Where did this Man [Jesus]
get this wisdom ... ?"'*

(MATTHEW 13:54B NKJV)

The ancient proverb writers urged men and women to 'Get wisdom;
get insight' (Proverbs 4:5 RSV). '[Wisdom] is more precious than
rubies' (Proverbs 3:15; 8:11 KJV). It obviously something urgently
needed and to be highly prized – both for salvation and service. 'The
fear of the LORD is the beginning of wisdom' (Proverbs 9:10).

All the wisdom writers in the Old Testament assure us that true
wisdom comes from God (Job 12:13; Proverbs 2:6; Ecclesiastes
2:26). It is God's wisdom we are called to seek after.[1]

WISDOM FOR LIVING AND LEADING

Today's leaders often represent the younger generation, pop-stars, sportspersons and celebrities. The media seek them out, listen to them and quote them extensively. Alexandr Solzhenitsyn, when he came to the West, gave a warning comment, 'It is against the natural order of things for those who are the youngest, with the least experience in life to have the greatest influence in directing the life of society.[2]

We would not expect to find wisdom in the politicians who surround themselves today with soundbites and spin-doctors. Our cynical world despises their 'wisdom', the word itself is no longer 'cool'. Talk of wisdom is dismissed as irrelevant.

But every leader soon discovers how essential it is to get wisdom, although they may not always call it that, and wants to know where it can be found. The Beatles thought they might find it with their Eastern gurus. Real wisdom comes from God himself who assures those who seek him that they will find him:

> Counsel is mine, and sound wisdom. I [wisdom] am understanding, I have strength. By me kings reign, And rulers decree justice. By me princes rule, and nobles, All the judges of the earth. I love those who love me, And those who seek me diligently will find me. (Proverbs 8:14–17 NKJV)

WHAT IS WISDOM?

It is the faculty for making the best use of knowledge. The modern generation may have the *facility* for *accessing* knowledge through their use of technology in our 'homo-up-to-datum' age, but still lacks the *faculty* for *assessing* knowledge. Philip Baker describes it as, 'Knowledge is intake; wisdom is output'.

Wisdom comes with an accumulation of experiences, which is why the Apostle Paul encouraged his church plants to appoint to leadership elders of good repute. Lack of relevant life experience, understanding, knowing where to turn or who to turn to, means it is often hard to know how to approach a given situation, especially for the church leaders.

God's wisdom is available from three areas.

1. The wisdom within us

People operate out of natural wisdom that develops with the years. We are all born with complex internal systems for computing the interaction of various gut feelings – common sense (widely dispensed but not evenly assigned), conscience, emotion, instinct, intuition, and a memory bank of past experiences, including pre-natal ones. These sensors cut across the routine thought processes and frequently leap straight from problem to answer. They seem to interact spontaneously in some subconscious epicentre of the human soul and then infuse their computed supra-rational response into our conscious thinking. This is a happy *modus operandi* for most of us most of the time, but in leadership situations it needs to be double-checked. After all, we usually want to be able to explain our decisions.

These sensors may help leaders to resonate and empathise with their followers at the visceral level; the downside, however, is that we all have our own hidden agendas made up of unmet needs from infancy, or other irrational beliefs that can easily cloud our perceptions. The result is that whilst we imagine we are exercising good judgement, in practice we may simply be giving rein to personal prejudices, or cultural preference, and possibly even latent jealousy, bigotry or some other bias. Clearly our gut feelings are better measured against some outside criteria. We need to test them against the wisdom of others (especially those older), if we are to communicate our objectives and plans convincingly enough for others to become involved.

2. The wisdom around us

The realisation that we are dependent upon other sources of wisdom has developed in each of us since birth. From our first breath we found comfort and security through the wise responses of our parents, and later from teachers and elders (those with more experience of life). Proverbs 11:14 and 24:6 teaches us that 'In the multitude of counsellors there is safety.' But, as we grow up into our teens, we find that we are increasingly inclined to ignore them. Though some of their advice may remain residually with us, we prefer to consult our siblings and teenage peers to give us the counsel we prefer.. This can often be to our disadvantage, as in the tragic case of the young King Rehoboam who 'rejected the advice which the elders had given him, and consulted the young men who had grown up with him, who stood before him' (1 Kings 12:8 NKJV).

Our sources of natural wisdom may also get distorted, not just by our peers, but by sensuality, deceiving spirits, and self-seeking, which obscure objectivity and lead to confusion (James 3:14).

But there is still another reliable resource readily available to us which is:

3. The wisdom above us

We have been encouraged by Scripture to ask of God when we lack wisdom (James 1:5). This is the wisdom from above. It is 'pure, then peaceable, gentle, willing to yield, full of mercy and good fruits, without partiality and without hypocrisy' (James 3:17 NRSV). This is why the book of Proverbs (4:7) claims that wisdom is the principal thing.

This kind of revealed wisdom has been handed down to us indirectly in the wisdom literature. We have the book of Job, the book of Proverbs and the book of Ecclesiastes recorded for us in Holy Scripture, where there is also so much of the wise teaching of Jesus and his followers.

God reveals his wisdom directly to individuals as well. This may be through an angel, a voice, a dream, a vision, a trance or a charism of the Holy Spirit – a word of wisdom, a prophecy or the discerning of spirits (1 Corinthians 12:7–11). God's wisdom is rarely revealed as an absolutely clear directive, though there is usually enough to discern the gist of what God's will is. In the end we are called to live by faith and we may still have to act without being absolutely certain. As businessman Lee Iacocca puts it:

> You never get all the facts. If you wait, by the time you do get them, your facts will be out of date because the market has moved on ... At some time, you know you have to take the *leap of faith* ... because even the right decision is wrong if it is made too late.

QUOTES
- Some people are so heavenly minded that they are no earthly use. (Anon)
- You don't need a weatherman to tell you which way the wind is blowing. (Bob Dylan)

- Wisdom is the practical side of moral goodness. (J. I. Packer)
- For every pound of learning a person may have, he needs ten pounds of common sense to know how to use it. (Persian Proverb)
- Many an institution is very well managed but poorly led. It may excel in ability to handle each day all the routine inputs yet may never ask whether the routine should be done at all. (Warren Bennis)
- Intuition is our capacity for direct knowledge, for immediate insight without observation or reason. (David G. Myers)
- There is no substitute for personal experience when it comes to dealing with problems. (Rudolph Giuliani)
- A wise man learns by the experience of others. An ordinary man learns by his own experience. A fool learns by nobody's experience. (Anon)
- Wisdom gained from one's personal experience provides a head start. (Rudolph Giuliani)
- I did the ordinary things that ordinary managers do. But on the whole I am far above the ordinary. (Malcolm Allison)
- Those who tell you it's tough at the top have never been at the bottom. (Joe Harvey)
- Winning is easy. It's far harder, once you've won, to lose honourably. I suppose I'll be beaten eventually. I only hope I accept it graciously. (Rodney Pattison)
- Winning is a drug. Once you have experienced it, you cannot do without it. You live for it. (Bernard Hunt)
- Wisdom is dynamic and grows in the using. (Christopher Cocksworth)
- It was wisdom that broke the categories of human thinking with the extravagance of God's grace. (Christopher Cocksworth)
- I fancy many would have arrived at wisdom if they had not fancied they had already arrived. (Seneca)
- Wisdom does not run with the crowd. (Philip Baker)
- The art of being wise is the art of knowing what to overlook. (William James)
- Where is the wisdom we have lost in our knowledge? (T. S. Eliot)
- True wisdom is a loving rationality. (Richard Foster)

- He stores up wisdom for the righteous (Proverbs 2:7).
- Intuition, that strange instinct that tells a woman she is right when she is not. (Anon)
- So teach us to number our days aright, that we may gain a heart of wisdom (Psalm 90:12 NIV).
- We can be knowledgeable with other men's knowledge but we cannot be wise with other men's wisdom. (Michael de Montaigne)
- Wisdom denotes the pursuing of the best ends by the best means. (Francis Hutchinson)
- Knowledge is proud that he has learned so much; wisdom is humble that he knows so little. (William Cowper)
- Experience is the comb life gives us after we have lost our hair. (Philip Baker)
- Man can know nothing except by going from the known to the unknown. (Anon)
- Many an institution is very well managed, but poorly led... In may excel in ability to handle each day all the routine inputs, yet may never ask whether the routine should be done at all. (Warren Bennis)

ILLUSTRATIONS
What to pray for your leader
Occasionally people graciously ask how they can pray for me. My response is the same every time: 'Please pray that I will have wisdom. Please pray that my leadership will be characterised by godly sober-mindedness. Please pray that I will discern God's mind on every matter.' (Bill Hybels)

Wisdom in a saint
St Francis of Assisi was committed to living out the cross in every aspect of his life and is a radical example of the sort of costly discipleship that is called for in living the gospel. In his dealings with people he showed an extraordinary, selfless wisdom that other people often found astonishing, but strangely convincing. A formative moment came well before he heard God call him to 'rebuild the church'.

Sometime after his conversion, as he was praying, he heard God saying, 'All the things you used to love after the flesh, and desired to have, you must now hate and despise if you would do my will. If you begin to do this, the things which seemed sweet and delightful before will be bitter and intolerable to you. And those things which you used to shrink from will give you an immeasurable sweetness.'

Encouraged by this word, Francis resumed his journey and very soon met a person with leprosy along the road. Leprosy in the medieval period was as much feared and hated as it was in biblical times and Francis had a particular loathing for the disease and its sufferers. But forcing himself to dismount, he gave the leprosy sufferer some money.

Then, compelled by the love of Christ, Francis found himself embracing him and kissing him. As he did so he found himself meeting Christ in that touch. Radical following of the way of the cross became the mark of his life and ministry. From then on people with leprosy became the special object of his compassion and Francis learnt that Christ is to be found by living in the way that Christ lived.

Throughout his life Francis seems to have heard God telling him to do things which did not fit the wisdom of the world or even the current wisdom of the church. They were the sort of apparently foolish things that made his own father distraught. You can almost hear his father saying to Francis, 'Look, I've given you every benefit in life including a good education and a professional training as a soldier and this is how you live your life.' The wisdom of the cross is foolishness to the world.[3]

Wisdom during the Great Depression

Get wisdom from wherever God has it waiting for you. When the Great Depression hit Wall Street, J. P. Morgan called in one expert after another, seeking opinions and advice.

'Why don't you tell them what to do, Mr Morgan?' his secretary asked him finally.

'I don't know what to do myself,' he said, 'but one day someone will come up with a plan that I know will work and then I will tell them what to do.'[4]

Wisdom from perseverance

Louisa Young is a rationalist who knows that the heart is just a pump. 'And yet,' she muses, 'it is the home of love and courage, and religion, and the soul, and almost any other human feeling you care to think of.'

Modern science tells us that these emotions are really chemical reactions fizzing within the human skull. But people from all continents and cultures have believed that the essence of individual identity lies in the heart, not in the head. Wondering why this should be she writes a fascinating book, *The Book of the Heart*, divided into four chambers: the *anatomist's* heart, the *religious* heart, the heart in *art* and the *lover's* heart.

DANGER OF SUBJECTIVE VIEWS

Tell people they are looking at the picture of a Gestapo officer and viewers will comment on obvious hints of cruelty in his tight lips and his unsmiling blue eyes. Tell them it is the photo of a resistance martyr and they will detect the clear signs of heroism in his face and brave traces of daring in the angle of his chin!

Life without wisdom

Actual excerpts from a 'Dear Abby' agony aunt column:

> Dear Abby,
> I have a man I never could trust. He cheats so much I'm not sure this baby I carry is his!

> Dear Abby,
> I've been going steady with this man for six years. We see each other every night. He says he loves me, and I know I love him, but he never mentions marriage. Do you think he's going out with me just for what he can get? Gertie.

> Dear Gertie,
> I don't know. What is he getting?

> Dear Abby,
> I suspected that my husband had been fooling around, and when I confronted him with the evidence he denied everything and said it would never happen again.

Dear Abby,
I am a 23-year-old liberated woman who has been on the pill for two years. It's getting expensive and I think my boyfriend should share half the cost but I don't know him well enough to discuss money with him.

Wisdom protects from being conned

Beware! Don't be taken in by what everyone is saying. Lt. Chris Argyris was a Signal Corps officer in charge of a depot near the end of World War II. When his tour was nearly over, a woman named Sheila called him out of his office, where about 300 employees had gathered. 'Lieutenant,' she said, 'we just want to tell you what a wonderful boss you have been.' Then she hugged and kissed him and gave him a savings bond in an envelope and a beautiful leather bag. He said he thought he must have been a pretty fine leader.

Sometime later, he went back to the depot to say hello. The war was over, and the man who had been his assistant was now running the place. Fishing for the 'warm fuzzy' of a compliment, he said 'Bill, tell me, what did you really think of me as a leader?' And Bill began to tell him negative things he had never heard before – that he was too competitive, that he didn't give a darn who he rolled over as long as he met the promised goals. He was stunned. Suddenly Sheila came their way.

'Sheila!' he called out to her. 'What Bill is saying about my leadership – is it true?'

She looked him straight in the face. 'Uh-huh, lieutenant, it sure is,' she said. 'And one more thing – all of us here are glad that the war finally ended because we were fed up with the act we had put on for all you officers.'

His immediate reaction was, 'Oh. This is so unfair!' But gradually he began to realise that whether the feedback was right or wrong, what was relevant was how *unaware* he had been. (Confession of Chris Argyris, a professor at Harvard Business School, Boston.)

BIBLICAL QUOTE

'Take heed to yourself and to the doctrine. Continue in them, for in doing this you will save both yourself and those who hear you.' (1 Timothy 4:16 NKJV)

A wise word from the heart of a leader
Our deepest fear
is not that we are inadequate.
Our deepest fear
is that we are powerful beyond measure.
It is our light, not our darkness,
that frightens us.
We ask ourselves, 'Who am I to be brilliant,
gorgeous, talented and fabulous?'
Actually who are you not to be?
You are a child of God.
Your playing small doesn't serve the world.
There is nothing enlightened
about shrinking so that other people
won't feel insecure around you.
We were born to make manifest
the glory of God that is within us.
It is not just in some of us; it's in everyone.
And as we let our own light shine,
we unconsciously give other people
permission to do the same.
As we are liberated from our fears,
our presence automatically liberates others.
                    (Nelson Mandela)

Biblical wisdom for any leader
Who is like a wise man?
And who knows the interpretation of a thing?
A man's wisdom makes his face shine,
And the sternness of his face is changed.
I say, 'Keep the king's commandment for the sake of your oath to God. Do not be hasty to go from his presence. Do not take your stand for an evil thing, for he does whatever pleases him.'
Where the word of a king is, there is power;
And who may say to him,
'What are you doing?'
He who keeps his command will experience nothing harmful;
And a wise man's heart discerns both time and judgment,
Because for every matter there is a time and judgment,

Though the misery of man increases greatly.
For he does not know what will happen;
So who can tell him when it will occur?
No one has power over the spirit to retain the spirit
And no one has power in the day of death.
There is no release from that war
and wickedness will not deliver those who are given to it.
All this I have seen, and applied my heart to every work that is done
under the sun: There is a time in which one man rules over another
to his own hurt.

(Ecclesiastes 8:1–9 NKJV)

PRAYERS

God, grant me the serenity to accept the things I cannot change,
courage to change the things I can, and the wisdom to know the
difference.

Gracious and Holy Father,
Give me the wisdom to perceive you, intelligence to understand you,
diligence to seek you,
patience to wait for you,
eyes to behold you,
heart to meditate upon you,
and life to proclaim you.
Through the power of the Holy Spirit of Jesus Christ, our Lord.

(St Benedict c.480–547)

Father you have promised to give wisdom generously
To all who ask by faith,
Please give me wisdom.
Make me wise to know your way for me,
Wise to make good decisions,
Wise to mentor others,
And wise to understand your word.
Through Jesus Christ my Lord. Amen. (Anon)

CHAPTER 7

People of humility, service and sacrifice

A Christian leader, like his Master, is a humble servant, not lording it over the flock like the leaders of this world.

(LUKE 22:25)

The way to up is down.

(DR DONALD BARNHOUSE)

When Michael Baughan became the Bishop of Chester he always carried a towel in his pocket to remind him of the servant role in the upper room.

LEADERSHIP CHARACTER

Jesus was looking for servant leaders, not self-serving leaders.

> When a leader is controlled by his self-serving his identity is determined by whether he wins or loses. ... Self-serving leaders, led by their egos, care about gaining and maintaining power status and position. (Ken Blanchard)

Jesus modelled quite the opposite for his disciples as the prophet Isaiah had foretold (Isaiah 42:1–4; 49:3–7; 52:13 – 53:12). His utter self-giving exemplified what he expected of his followers. St Paul summed it up superbly when he wrote, 'Taking the form of a servant, and coming in the likeness of men, ... he humbled himself and became obedient to the point of death, even death on a cross' (Philippians 2:7,8). And this humble man proved to be the greatest leader of all time, greater than Moses, Alexander the Great, Mohammed, Napoleon, or Abraham Lincoln. Christ is 'the supreme transformer of all time' (Michael Green). He exemplified sheer goodness, he taught the values of God's kingdom, and he trained disciples to do the same, well-knowing the cost to himself but prepared to pay the price, whatever the personal sacrifice.

History never hid his humility.

> He came from a small village, a humble background, came to birth in a manner generally believed to be of questionable legitimacy. He had little formal education; he never fought a military battle, never wrote a book, had no home of his own and was executed at the age of thirty-three. Yet he still transforms people of all nationalities from all over the world today, 2,000 years after his death and resurrection. (Michael Green)

His followers currently constitute the fastest growing faith community on earth. There have been more Christian believers living during this last decade, greater than the sum total of Christians in the entire history of the Church up to the year 1990. So high has been their commitment that these followers have been, and still are, ready to die for his cause. Indeed today it is reckoned that somewhere in the world one Christian is martyred every two minutes.

THE GREAT VICE
One of the greatest temptations that a leader faces is pride – such an ugly and dangerous thing. 'Pride goes before a fall.' Solomon warned: 'When pride comes, then comes shame' (Proverbs 11:2 NKJV). C. S. Lewis called pride 'The Great Vice' and described it as 'something we see in everyone else but never in ourselves'. It's the only disease that makes everyone sick except the one who has it. 'Pride is like a man's shirt – it's the first thing on and the last thing off.' A proud man strides through life looking down on other people and things. Lewis observed that a man looking down doesn't see things above himself. He doesn't see God.

Leadership takes one to a position of power and therefore leaders are much more susceptible to the processes of this particular temptation. To be in a place of power is to be in a place of peril. Lord Acton astutely observed, 'Power corrupts and absolute power corrupts absolutely.'

St Paul once shared with the church how he sought to humble

himself constantly – 'I die daily' (1 Corinthians 15:31 KJV). It was with this in mind, no doubt, that he also wrote discouraging others from exalting him as their leader. 'I am the least of the apostles' (1 Corinthians 15:9 KJV) he asserted in one form or another: '[I am] the least of all saints' (Ephesians 3:8 KJV); 'I am the chief of sinners' (1 Timothy 1:15).

HUMBLE, AND PROUD OF IT
In one of his classics,[1] C. S. Lewis describes how Screwtape, a high-ranking demon, teaches his nephew Wormwood how he might easily trip up a young Christian.

> 'Try to inflate the subject's pride,' he writes. 'Your patient has become humble; have you drawn his attention to the fact? All virtues are less formidable to us once the man is aware that he has them, but this is specially true of humility. Catch him at the moment when he is really poor in spirit, and smuggle into his mind the gratifying reflection, "By Jove! I'm being humble," and almost immediately pride – pride at his own humility – will appear. If he awakes to the danger and tries to smother this new form of pride, make him proud of his attempt – and so on, through as many stages as you please.'

The objective for any leader, as the Americans say, is to 'get small' and then to keep small. The more low-key and laid-back the leader's attitude and style, the better. Even though the leader may have to be visible he can always be self-effacing and gently deflect credit towards others in the leadership team, speaking little of his own part.

Truly the way to up is down. (Donald Barnhouse)

QUOTES
- The one who rules should be like the one who serves. (Jesus)
- Moses, one of the greatest leaders of all time was renowned for his meekness which was not to be confused for weakness. (Anon)
- The Kingdom of God is an 'upside down' Kingdom. Heavens values are often the complete reversal of those of this world. (Anon)
- If leaders have to give up to go up, then they have to give up

more to stay up. (John Maxwell)
- It's not titles but towels that mark a good leader. (Anon)
- Leaders need the paradoxical combination of arrogance and humility to succeed. (Anon)
- I have often had to eat my words, and I must confess that I have always found it a wholesome diet. (Winston Churchill)
- People with humility don't think less of themselves ... they think about themselves less. (Bill Hybels)
- Think as little as possible about yourself. Turn your eyes resolutely from any view of your influence, your success, your following. Above all speak as little as possible about yourself' (Samuel Wilberforce)
- Great men never think they are great – small men never think they are small. (Anon)
- The true secret of spiritual strength is self-distrust and deep humility. (J. C. Ryle)
- He who knows himself best esteems himself least. (Henry G. Bohn)
- Until a man is nothing God can make nothing of him. (Martin Luther)
- No man has ever risen to the real stature of spiritual manhood until he has found that it is finer to serve somebody else than it is to serve himself. (Woodrow Wilson)

ILLUSTRATIONS
The supreme example
In your relationships with one another, have the same attitude of mind Jesus had. Who, being in the very nature of God, did not consider equality with God something to be used to his own advantage; rather he made himself nothing by taking the very nature of a servant, being made in human likeness, and being found in appearance as a human being, he humbled himself by becoming obedient to death – even death on a cross! (cf Philippians 2:5–8)

Have we NO RIGHTS?

On the mission field it is not the enduring of hardship, the lack of comforts, and the roughness of life that make the missionary cringe and falter. It is something far less romantic and far more real. It is something that will hit you right down where you live. The missionary will have to give up having his own way. He has to give up having any rights. He has, in the words of Jesus, to 'deny himself'. He just has to give up himself.

Paul knew all about this ... 'Have we no right to eat and to drink?' he asks. 'Have we not a right to forbear working? ... Nevertheless', he goes on, 'we did not use this right ... though I was free from all men, I brought myself under bondage to all, that I might gain the more' (1 Corinthians 9:4,6,12,19). Paul, as a missionary, willingly gave up his rights for the sake of the gospel. 'But someone will ask, 'Why should this be especially true for the *missionary*? Do not the same principles apply to the church leader, and indeed to any true believer in Jesus Christ?'[2] (Mabel Williamson)

A life of humility

He was born in an obscure village, the child of a peasant woman.
He grew up in still another village, where he worked in a carpenter shop until he was thirty.
Then for three years he was an itinerant preacher.
He never wrote a book.
He never held an office.
He never had a family or owned a house
He didn't go to college.
He never travelled more than 200 miles from the place where he was born.
He did none of the things one usually associates with greatness.
He had no credentials but himself.
He was only 33 when public opinion turned against him.
His friends ran away.
He was turned over to his enemies and went through the mockery of a trial.
He was nailed to a cross between two thieves.
When he was dying, his executioners gambled for his clothing, the only property he had on earth.
When he was dead, he was laid in a borrowed grave through the pity of a friend.

Nineteen centuries have come and gone, and today he is the central figure of the human race. The leader of mankind's progress.

All the armies that ever marched, all the navies that ever sailed, all the parliaments that ever sat, all the kings that ever reigned, put together, have not affected the life of man on earth as much as that One Solitary Life. (Anon)

An old priest

James Ryle tells of a dream he once had of an imposing cathedral into which he was led. He found there a cranky old priest with a face like a wrinkled prune. This man looked up at Ryle and snapped at him, 'What do you want?' whereupon Ryle took him by the hand and replied: 'Follow me'.

The old priest rose from his chair and walked with Ryle down to the first floor. As they descended the steps, the old priest began to turn young again. The lower we went, the more youthful and radiant he became. He started whistling, and finally began singing aloud of his love for Jesus. Arriving at the first floor Ryle heard a voice say, 'The secret of happiness is servanthood. Your youth will be renewed like the eagle as you humble yourself and return to your first love, serving the Lord with gladness.'[3]

Preparation for service

When God intends to fill a soul, he first makes it empty.
When he intends to enrich a soul, he first makes it poor.
When he intends to exalt a soul, he first makes it sensible to its own miseries, wants and nothingness. (John Flavel)

Beware of self-glorification

Charles Spurgeon once exhorted the students at his college, 'We have plenty of people nowadays who could not kill a mouse without publishing it in the Gospel Gazette. Samson killed a lion and said nothing about it; the Holy Spirit finds modesty so rare that He takes care to record it. Say much of what the Lord has done for you but say little of what you have done for the Lord. Do not utter a self-glorifying sentence.'[4]

When the athlete tripped

At the Special Olympics the nine finalists in the 100 yard dash prepared for the start of the race. When the gun went off, these contestants, with various disabilities, headed down the track toward the finishing line. Part way down one of the competitors fell. He tried to get up, but fell again. He tried again, but without success.

One by one the other contestants stopped and all headed back towards him. When they reached him they lifted him up and all nine contestants walked down the track holding hands and crossed the finishing line together. The crowd could not believe it and rose to their feet to give them a 15-minute standing ovation.[5]

Generals absent from the firing line
Peter Drucker tells how in the mid 1920s his class had to read up about the Great War and find out why so many researchers viewed it as *a war of total military incompetence*. After the class had discussed why this might be, their teacher, a wounded war veteran himself, finally shared his own view: 'Not enough generals were killed; they stayed way behind the lines and let others do the dying.'

This led Drucker to observe that:

> Effective leaders may have to delegate a number of things but they must never delegate the one thing they can do with excellence, the one thing that will make a difference, the one thing that will set the standards, the one thing they want to be remembered for.

He was talking about personal sacrifice for the cause.[6]

Advice from King Attila the Hun
A chieftain should dress in fine skins and furs, not those draped by gold and silver adornments. Pompous appearance breeds hate and gives rise to contempt and laughter among the ranks. (King Attila the Hun)

Why did he do that?
Barry Kissell once told the story of how he went with John Perry (later the Bishop of Chelmsford) to play squash. Returning after the game, they saw to their disgust that someone had been sick all over the changing room floor and had not cleaned it up. John's immediate comment was quite simple, 'Oh dear, we had better clear that up!'

And then proceeded to do so.

Willing to do the dirty job

Jesus did not want his disciples to be leaders first. He wanted them to be servants first. (Mark 9:35b) A missionary in South America was told of a new recruit coming out to serve in Chile and mentioned that she had known him at college.

'What's he like?' the rest of us asked.

'Oh he'll do well here,' she said, and explained how that at college whenever a volunteer was needed for some kind of humble service this new recruit had always been the first to volunteer his help!

The narrow ledge

There is a story attributed to Martin Luther of two mountain goats that met each other on a narrow ledge just wide enough for one of the animals to pass. On one side was a sheer cliff, and on the other a steep wall of rock. These two goats came face to face and it was impossible for either to turn or to back up. Had they been humans, they would probably have started butting each other until one of them plunged to its death down into the deep chasm below. But according to Luther, the goats had more sense than that. One of them simply lay down on the trail and let the other literally walk over him. Both were able to continue safely on their way!

Look out for humility

The Venerable Bede, (c 673–735), Britain's earliest historian, relates how Pope Gregory I sent Augustine as an abbot with some other monks to England to preach the faith to the Saxons and Angles who had been neglected by the Celts. God blessed his mission and a number were converted. The English king Ethelbert was pleased with him and invited Augustine and his monks to settle in Canterbury. Augustine was called to Arles to be consecrated a bishop by order of the Pope.

When Augustine returned to Britain he invited the Celtic bishops to meet him. The Celts were puzzled about his motives and asked a wise hermit whether they should submit to Augustine or not.

'Yes,' said the old hermit, 'if he is a man of God.'

'How can we tell?' they replied.

'You will know if he is gentle and humble of heart.'

Still perplexed they asked, 'How can we discern that about him?'

The hermit suggested that they arrange for Augustine and his men to arrive first at their meeting place. 'If he [the bishop] stands up when you arrive, it will prove that he is a servant of Christ. In that case do as he bids.'

Apparently Augustine failed to rise when he greeted the Celts and they remained reticent about accepting his leadership.

No room for egos
There are no big egos around the England camp because he has no ego himself. I love watching him work. He makes the game simple. His explanations are not cluttered with detail. He gets his message across with a minimum of complications and players respond ... he pricks the balloon of his own bombast and presumption before anyone else can get near.[7] (Ron Draper)

Pride is easily offended
Lady Huntingdon invited the Duchess of Buckingham to hear George Whitfield preach. The Duchess replied:

> I thank your ladyship for the information concerning the Methodist preacher; their doctrines are most repulsive, strongly tinctured with Impertinence & Disrespect towards their Superiors, in perpetually endeavouring to level all Ranks, and do away with all Distinctions. It is monstrous to be told that you have a heart as sinful as the common wretches that crawl the Earth. This is highly offensive and insulting; and I cannot but wonder that your Ladyship should relish any Sentiment so much at variance with High Rank and Good Breeding.

Arrogance
One of the most destructive traits a leader can have today is arrogance – acting like you've got it together all the time. On the other hand one of the most endearing qualities a leader can have is to be in touch with his or her own vulnerability. It's that side of a leader that keeps the vision from crumbling under pressure of circumstances. (Ken Blanchard and Don Shula, *The Little Book of Coaching*)

Godly counsel
God protecteth the humble and delivereth him; the humble He loveth and comforteth; unto the humble man He inclineth himself; unto the humble He giveth great grace; and after his humiliation He raiseth him to glory. Unto the humble He revealeth His secrets, and sweetly draweth and inviteth him unto Himself (Thomas à Kempis, *Of the Imitation of Christ*)

Prayer
Lord, please help me to crucify my pride and humble my spirit before you are compelled to humiliate me for my own good and the sake of your kingdom. (Anon)

CHAPTER 8

People who have enthusiasm

*Enthusiasm provides 'the capacity and will to rally men
and women to a common purpose, and the character which
will inspire confidence. The leader must have infectious optimism
and the determination to persevere in the face of difficulties.
He must radiate confidence.'*
(FIELD MARSHAL MONTGOMERY)

He won 2,748 races, with nothing but fire in his belly.[1]
(SAID OF A 19TH CENTURY FLAT RACE JOCKEY, FRED ARCHER)

Don't Fire Them - Fire Them Up.[2]
(FRANK PACETTA)

*Are the Christians in this church 'on fire'? Do they live committed
lives and practice their faith with joy and enthusiasm?*
(CHRISTIAN A. SCHWARZ - ENTHUSIASM APPEARS TO BE ONE OF EIGHT
BASIC QUALITIES FOUND IN HEALTHY GROWING CHURCHES)

Literally enthusiasm means 'God-breathed'.
(PHILIP KING)

UPSIDE OF ENTHUSIASM

Enthusiasm is often regarded as immature. Sometimes it is. But it's also too easy to grow cynical and lose whatever enthusiasm we might have had, and in the process quench the keen spirit of those around us. Enthusiasm is a vital element in a leader's kit list; it is a wholesome gift of God to be highly prized if one has it.

A leader has to be a self-starter and that is where enthusiasm kicks in. Enthusiasm inspires vision, optimism and energy. Enthusiasm gets things done. Another word for enthusiasm is passion. Schwarz calls it 'passionate spirituality'. As opposed to indifference and boredom, passion invites everyone who wants to join in the dance of life to make their dreams come true. When people enjoy what they are doing they do it better.

Others quickly notice if the leader's heart is not in his work. Enthusiasm helps the leader to put zest in his style, and a buzz among his people. In a recent letter of resignation, government minister Michael Wills wrote to the Prime Minister saying: 'Politics has always, in the end, got to be about passion, and that flows from a very clear sense of what your values are.' We remember, at the beginning of the Second World War, how Winston Churchill, against all the odds, inspired the British nation by his enthusiasm.

Moods are, quite literally, contagious. Enthusiastic leadership is the spark that ignites a team's performance, creating a landscape of success or a bonfire of ashes. Moods matter greatly. 'A cranky and ruthless boss creates a toxic organisation of negative achievers; [while] an upbeat and inspirational leader spawns acolytes for whom any challenge is surmountable.[3]

DOWNSIDE OF ENTHUSIASM

Every upside has its downside, and the downside of enthusiasm is that it can lead to fanaticism. Before his conversion to Christ, Paul had directed his religious zeal into cruel persecution of the church, (Philippians 3:6).

Zeal needs tempering otherwise it becomes carnal, unloving, insensitive and irrational. A God-given enthusiast in the service of Jesus Christ must not only have the fire of God in his belly but the love of God in his heart. It also needs to be recognised that passion alone is no reflection of loyalty to the truth; many false sects have been spread by heretical enthusiasts.

SELF-CONTROL

All emotion demands self-control.

> 'From my childhood days,' wrote Rudolph Giuliani, 'I had trained myself to control my emotions when others became more emotional. My father had always told me to remain calm in a crisis. As others around me got excited, he said, staying deliberately calm would help me figure out the right answers.

When a crisis occurred, it was my job to lead people through it. That certainly did not mean I didn't have feelings. Of course I did. And it didn't mean I wouldn't show what I was feeling. Of course I could. Leaders are human, and it actually helps the people you lead to realise that.'

QUOTES

- The zeal for my father's house shall consume me. (John 2:17)
- Nothing great was ever achieved without enthusiasm. (Ralph Waldo Emerson)
- The most influential leaders in history, the social reformers and pioneers have been men and women of action because they have been the men and women of thought and passion. (John Stott)
- You have to touch a heart before you can ask a hand. (John C. Maxwell)
- And hence one master passion in the breast, like Aaron's serpent swallows up the rest. (Alexander Pope)
- Enthusiasm is the greatest business asset in the world. (Anon)
- Success is moving from one failure to another with enthusiasm. (Winston Churchill)
- Smile and the world smiles with you.
- Zeal without knowledge is a sister of Folly: But though it be witless, men hold it most holly [holy]. (John Davies, *The Scourge of Folly*, 1611)
- Good leaders are optimists. Pessimists do not usually make good leaders. (Anon)
- Optimism is true moral courage. (Sir Ernest Shackleton)
- The purpose of this meeting is to fire you with enthusiasm. If it doesn't, I shall fire you -.with enthusiasm. (Frank Paceta, Manager of a Sales Department)
- People can succeed at almost anything for which they have enthusiasm. (Anon)
- In loving Memory of our Vicar, who successfully resisted enthusiasm for over forty years. (Plaque on UK church wall)
- Fervour and Anglicanism are almost a contradiction in

terms. (Alan Bennett)

- Modern theology is 'flat tyre' religion. All the pneuma has gone out of it. (Marcus Borg)
- I consider my ability to arouse enthusiasm among people the greatest asset I possess. (Anon)
- Those who dare, do; those who dare not, do not. (Anon)
- If you keep on saying things are going to be bad, you have a good chance of being a prophet. (Isaac Bashevis Singer)
- Always borrow money from a pessimist: he doesn't expect to get it back again! (Anon)

ILLUSTRATIONS
Enthusiasm ignites passion.
He [Kevin Spacey] exudes a passionate enthusiasm mixed with a kind of awed delight as he contemplates his task when, next year, he becomes the troubled theatre's artistic director.[4] (John Hiscock)

Enthusiasm intimidated by fear
Melburn McBroom was a domineering boss, with a temper that intimidated those working with him. McBroom was an airline pilot. One day in 1978 McBroom's plane was approaching Portland, Oregon, when he noticed a problem with the landing gear. So McBroom went into a holding pattern, circling the field at a high altitude while he tried adjusting parts of the mechanism.

While McBroom continued to be obsessed over the landing gear, the plane's fuel gauges were steadily approaching the empty level. But his co-pilots were so fearful of McBroom's wrath that they said nothing, even as disaster loomed. The plane crashed killing ten people. The story of that crash is still told as a cautionary tale in the safety of airline pilots.[5] (Daniel Goleman)

Enthusiasm involves intensity
Intensity is measured by a person's level of will and passion to do whatever it takes to get the job done successfully. The intensity to strive for continual improvement matters as never before in today's business world ... Any level of successful leadership demands the same level of consistent intensity that led Don Shula to become the National Football League's winning coach. His first win in 1975 was no different from his 325th in 1995.[6] (Ken Blanchard)

Enthusiasm exploits opportunity

Two salesmen were sent to a distant country to sell shoes for their business. Two days after arrival one of them realised that no one wore shoes at all and did not need them in that part of the world. He cabled home: 'Local inhabitants do not wear shoes. Please send return ticket urgently!'

The other man cabled head office: 'Local inhabitants have no shoes at all. Ship out 5,000 pairs urgently!'

Some saw Goliath as too big to master: David saw Goliath as too big to miss. (Anon)

Optimists and pessimists

Pessimists see the difficulties in every opportunity. Optimists see the opportunity in every difficulty. Pessimists burn their bridges before they cross them. Optimists cross their bridges before they burn them. Optimists tend to look at things positively. Pessimists tend to look at things negatively. The cautious pessimists however are God-given to challenge the audacious optimist. But we still need to be careful: while optimists can be dazzled by the promises of the future, pessimists can be blinded by the failures of the past.

Enthusiasm evokes vision

When John Constable, the landscape painter, wrote to a friend in 1821 that 'painting is but another name for feeling', he defined in seven words the essence of Romantic painting at the precise moment when that movement was being born.

These painters also changed the direction of French 19th-century art. Constable's *View on the Stour at Dedham* was exhibited in Lille in 1825. It was a shock to the popular neo-classicist painters such as Jacques Louis David and his followers on the other side of the Channel. What puzzled these more conservative French critics was that Constable chose to paint a nondescript corner of the English countryside, in his own words 'to make something out of nothing', instead of selecting a breathtaking vista, or one ennobled by its association with the ancient world.

The place of 'Romanticism' was being re-discovered in all the arts at that time. Feelings have their proper and very positive role in society.

Enthusiasm encourages buoyancy

Some leaders are not by nature cheerfully disposed, like Miguel de Cervantes' *Knight of the Sorrowful Countenance*, and may also have depressive temperaments. But it is possible to smile and impart good cheer to others even if one does not feel like it. Indeed it is vital for a leader to do so. That was one of the secrets of Mother Teresa's success. An Italian newspaper reflected on her recently published diaries:

> The real Mother Teresa was one who had visions for a year and who for the next fifty had doubts – right up until the time of her death. People were inspired by her sweet serenity and had no idea of her inner struggles with darkness and sense of self-worthlessness.[7]

Prime minister Winston Churchill was, all his life, subject to depression, his 'black dog', as he called it, but he still overcame it outwardly to inspire the nation to victory. Successful leaders have learned to do the same with their enthusiasm.

The second line of that great blessing which Aaron, the High Priest, was commanded to pronounce upon Israel in God's name runs, 'The Lord make his face to shine upon you' meaning may the Lord smile on you! To smile upon people is to bless people with your delight in them; it radiates a loving expression towards them and gives others confidence and hope. Enthusiasm keeps smiling.

Enthusiasm excites creativity

Beware of the destructive power of negative language. It will crush all creativity and quench any vision. As a small boy I was making a gun to defend myself against a possible German parachutist. The gun would never have worked but I wanted it to look and sound real. My eldest brother came by. He asked me what I was trying to make and listened to my reply. He must have been amused at my idea. Instead of mocking it however, he said how good it was and then suggested how I could make it even better if I did this and added that and painted something else. I never forgot that encouraging gesture!

Prayer

Dear Lord, put more fire in my belly and keep it burning. Amen.

CHAPTER 9

People who have integrity

'The just man walketh in his integrity:
his children are blessed after him.'
(PROVERBS 20:7 KJV)

In order to be a leader a man must have followers.
And to have followers a man must have their confidence.
Hence the supreme quality of a leader is unquestionably integrity.
His teachings and actions must square with each other.
(PRESIDENT DWIGHT D. EISENHOWER)

Captains have to work hard to maintain a standard: they have
to keep their committees happy, appease the supporters' clubs,
attend all the training sessions, study the opposition,
make diplomatic speeches and be above reproach themselves.
(J. G. THOMAS QUOTED IN RUGBY WORLD 1973)

In research conducted in 1995 into the most respected characteristic of an admired leader, 88 per cent said it was honesty.

THE NEED FOR INTEGRITY

Where there is no integrity, there is no credibility and without credibility there will soon be disillusionment and despair. A Nigerian novelist, Chinua Achebe, has currently critiqued his own country's lack of leadership: 'The Nigerian problem is the unwillingness or inability of its leaders to rise to the responsibility, or go to the challenge of personal example which are the hallmarks of true leadership.' He observed how leadership has tragically failed his own country through lack of integrity.

Jerry Rawlins, Ghana's former military dictator, said in a recent interview, 'Governing in Africa is like paddling in a canoe with a hole punched in it.' He expressed his disgust with the entrenched patronage and corrupt practices of so many African leaders. Of course we know of many other parts of the world where sadly the same comments would be true.

In Greek there is a word that means 'to chisel' or 'to carve out of stone, to hammer out'. The word 'character' is derived from that. It means willingness to take an unpopular position or make an unpopular decision because you know it's the right thing to do; you know it's the best long-term decision for everybody.

Sincerity
When Spanish craftsmen made faulty cuts in the marble they were working on, or the traders wanted to disguise some unsightly pitting, they would smooth off the surface with wax (*cera*) to deceive the inexperienced buyer. An expert looking for the best piece to buy would look for marble that was *sincera*, 'without wax', from which we get our word 'sincere'.

To have integrity is to be sincere, no deliberately disguised faults. No cover-ups. You are sincere when you are what you appear to be. Your words and your deeds match. A dictionary definition of integrity is 'the state of being complete, unified'. People with integrity are those who are who they are, no matter where they are or who they are with.

John Maxwell has observed that 'Integrity is not only the referee between two desires; it's the "decision maker" between being happy and being fragmented. It frees you to be the whole person no matter what comes your way.'

People with integrity are not divided (duplicitous) nor are they pretending (hypocritical). They have nothing to hide and nothing to fear. It is vital for leaders hoping to build integrity into a team to have the real thing in themselves. Followers quickly spot where this is missing. They are easily inspired when their leader is transparent. They are quickly disillusioned with a leader who is not. Christian integrity in leadership means living a life where other people can see through you, and better still when they see Christ in you.

St Paul urged the young Timothy in training for leadership 'to know himself and his doctrine'. Some leaders know their doctrine but have difficulty in recognising their own defects.

QUOTES

- 'Select capable men from all the people – men who fear God, trustworthy men who hate dishonest gain ...' (Exodus 18:21 NIV).
- 'I put in charge of Jerusalem my brother Hanani, along with Hananiah the commander of the citadel, because he was a man of integrity and feared God more than most men do' (Nehemiah 7:2 NIV).
- 'Teacher, we know that you are true, and ... do not regard the position of men, but truly teach the way of God.' (Mark 12:14b RSV).
- 'Woe to the shepherds of Israel who only take care of themselves! Should not shepherds take care of the flock? You eat the curds, clothe yourselves with the wool and slaughter the choice animals, but you do not take care of the flock. You have not strengthened the weak or healed the sick or bound up the injured. You have not brought back the strays or searched for the lost. You have ruled them harshly and brutally. So they were scattered because there was no shepherd' (Ezekiel 34:2–5 NIV).
- It is required of a steward that he be found faithful. (1 Corinthians 4:2)
- Victory if possible. Integrity at all costs. (Ken Blanchard)
- Effective leaders have high integrity and are clear and straightforward in their interactions with others. (Ken Blanchard)
- Integrity in everything precedes all else. (Max DePree)
- Leaders live in the public eye and perceptions of them soon become facts of life. (Anon)
- Integrity produces authenticity. (Anon)
- Followers adamantly demand that a leader possesses a high degree of integrity when it comes to self perception. (Max DePree)
- Champions don't become champions in the ring; they are merely recognised there. (Sporting Maxim)
- I would rather be right than be consistent. (Winston Churchill's comment when he had to change his mind)
- What you do speaks so loud, I can't hear what you say. (Anon)

- Every great institution is the lengthened shadow of a single man. His character determines the character of his organisation. (Ralph Waldo Emérson)
- The most effective leadership is by example not edict. (John Maxwell)
- I don't know any other way to lead but by example. (Don Shula)
- My worth to God in public is what I am in private. (Oswald Chambers)
- Integrity without knowledge is weak and useless but knowledge without integrity is dangerous and dreadful. (Samuel Johnson)
- Who you are is who you attract. (John Maxwell)
- A single lie destroys a whole reputation for integrity. (Balthasar Gracian)
- It's the easiest thing in the world for a man to deceive himself. (Benjamin Franklin)
- The key to greatness is to be in reality what we appear to be. (Socrates)
- The first step towards the recovery of our Christian integrity is to be aware that our culture blinds, deafens, and dopes us. (John Stott)
- When a leader knows where and what needs improvement he knows where to focus his attention. (Anon)
- Self-confidence is so often the enemy of self-knowledge. (Jeremy Paxman)
- Live so that the preacher can tell the truth at your funeral. (Anon)
- People may doubt what you say, but they will always believe what you do. (Anon)
- Exceptional leaders distinguish themselves because they know their strengths, their limits, and their weaknesses. (Daniel Coleman)
- I would rather be right, than President. (Henry Clay, when told he was risking his chances of being elected president)

ILLUSTRATIONS
Counsellors can help one to be accountable
Bill Hybels shares a painful experience when three wise advisors came to him on behalf of the vast church he had built up over many years.

'Bill,' they said, 'there were two eras during the first twenty years of Willow Creek's history, when, by your own admission, you were not at your leadership best, once in the late seventies and again in the early nineties. The data shows that Willow Creek paid dearly for your leadership fumble. It cost us all more than you'll ever know.'

They followed by saying, 'The best gift you can give the people you lead here … is a healthy, energized, fully surrendered, and focused self. And no one can make that happen in your life except you. It's up to you to make the right choices so you can do your best.'

While they were talking the Holy Spirit was telling me, 'They're right, Bill. They are right.'[1]

Building with both hands
He who gives good advice builds with one hand.
He who gives good counsel and example builds with both.
But he who gives good admonition and bad example builds with one hand and pulls down with the other. (Francis Bacon)

Business file
According to a recent survey, men say that the first thing they notice about women is their eyes. And women say the first thing they notice about men is that they are a bunch of liars!

Letter to the tax man
Dear Sir, I have been evading paying my taxes for years. Please find the enclosed money that I owe you. If I find that I am not sleeping better after this I will send the rest! (Sender Anonymous)

Isn't it awful!
Two elderly ladies visiting a country churchyard came across a headstone inscribed 'Here Lies Tom Smith, a Politician and an Honest Man'. 'Horrors!' one of them cried. 'Isn't it awful how they have had to put those two people together in the same grave!'

Secret sinning and public leading
In his aptly entitled book *Integrity: How I Lost It and My Journey*

Back, Richard Dortch shares how he served time in prison for shielding Jimmy Bakker, who had formerly had an extra-marital affair. Dortch evaded telling the truth about the money used to pay off the woman in order to save what he felt was the greater good of Heritage USA, a magnificent Christian project largely funded from gifts via Jimmy and Tammy Bakker's TV station.

He wrote, 'I became so intoxicated with the growth of Heritage USA, so enamoured with what was developing around me that I refused to see what was happening.' He later observed that 'in the many years he had served as a leader he had noticed that almost everyone who had fallen, both leader and layman, did so because they believed that *an exception would be made in their case*. They could pick and choose. They could sin … even if only occasionally … even for a good cause, and it would make no difference [to their Christian work and witness]. They could have a public persona and no one would ever see the other side of their life.[2]

Openness in champion sports coaches
Finally and maybe most importantly, champion coaches operate out of unquestionable integrity … They do not have hidden agendas. They do not say one thing and mean another. They do not manipulate people. They are genuine and sincere.

If you are honesty based, you will not waste energy trying to be what you are not, or try to cover your tracks because you keep telling people different stories. In fact only by being honesty-based can you sustain high performance. People who are not honesty-based lose the game of life, because they lose the trust of other people around them. And the moment you lose other people's trust you lose everything.[3]

Integrity in everything
An American soldier won the Croix de Guerre in France but refused to wear it.

'No! I was no good back at home. I let my sister and my widowed mother support me. I was a dead beat. This medal is for something I did here at the Front but I am not going to wear it here. I am going back home first to show my mother that I can make good at home and then I will.' (Quoted by Harry Emerson Fosdick)

Dangerous idealist who practised deception
He [Hayward] was a man who saw nothing for himself, but only

through a literary atmosphere, and he was dangerous because he had deceived himself into sincerity. He honestly mistook his sensuality for romantic emotion, his vacillation for artistic temperament and his idleness for philosophic charm. His mind, vulgar in its effort at refinement, saw everything a little larger than life-size, with the outlines blurred in a golden mist of sentimentality. He lied and never knew that he lied, and when it was pointed out to him, said that lies were beautiful. He was an idealist.[4]

Self-aggrandisement in the name of promoting another

In the Poets' Corner of Westminster Abbey there is a memorial to John Milton.

In the year of our Lord Jesus Christ
One thousand seven hundred and thirty seven
This bust
of the Author of Paradise Lost
was placed here by William Benson Esq.
One of the auditors of the Imprest
to His Majesty King George the Second,
formerly
Surveyor General of the Works
To his majesty King George the first
Rysbrack
was the statuary who cut it

This memorial to John Milton was really all about William Benson. He put it up as a device for personal self-aggrandisement. Milton is merely the excuse; the focus falls on Benson. He was using the name of a famous Puritan poet to parade himself before the public eye, and to get his name into the Abbey, not by his own distinction, but by riding in on the back of someone else's distinction.

Self-importance

Brother Yun, the young leader of a growing House Church Movement in Northern China, once again under the excruciating torture of his Chinese prison guards, believed he was learning a fundamental lesson in those most extreme circumstances:

In my proud heart I had been thinking that I was important to the Church and that they needed me to lead them. Now I vividly understood that he is God and I am but a feeble man. I realised that God did not need me at all and that if he ever chose to use me again it would be nothing more than a great privilege. (Brother Yun, *The Heavenly Man*)

What about the glory?

Chuck Colson, a lawyer known as President Nixon's hatchet man, had an experience of Christ that radically changed him and led him to a lifetime of service for others, especially prisoners. He relates the story of some young people who ventured out for an afternoon to find how they could serve others. They were from Shively Christian Church, led at the time by a Youth Pastor, Dave Stone, and they were fiercely competitive with their neighbour, Shively Baptist Church, especially in the area of sports.

One week the Bible lesson was about Jesus washing his disciples' feet (from John chapter 13). To drive home the lesson Pastor Stone divided them into groups and told them to go out and find a practical way to be servants.

'I want you to be Jesus in the city for the next two hours,' he said. 'If Jesus were here, what would he do? Figure out how he would help people.'

Two hours later the kids reconvened in Dave Stone's living room to report what they had done. One group had done two hours of yard work for an elderly man. Another group had bought ice cream treats and delivered them to several widows in the church. A third group visited a church member in the hospital. Another group went to a nursing home and sang Christmas carols etc.

When the fifth group stood up and reported what they had done everyone groaned. This group had made its way to none other than their arch-rival, Shively Baptist, where they had asked the pastor if he knew someone who needed help. The pastor sent them to the home of an elderly woman who needed garden work done. There for two hours, they mowed grass and forked over the garden etc, and when they were getting ready to leave, the woman called the group together and thanked them for their hard work. 'I don't know how I could get along without you,' she told them. 'You kids at Shively Baptist are always coming to my rescue.'

'Shively Baptist!' interrupted Dave Stone. 'I sure hope you set her straight, and told her that you were from Shively Christian Church!'

'Why no, we didn't,' they replied. 'We didn't think that mattered!'[5]

Checking one's own integrity

Answers to the following three questions will reveal whether we are into image-building or integrity development:

1. Are you the same no matter whom you're with?
2. Do you make decisions that are best for others, or when another choice would benefit you more?
3. Are you quick to recognise others for their efforts and their contributions to your success?

Open honesty

President Lincoln had been given some very depressing news by his Secretary for War about the disloyalty of many who had been considered Unionist supporters. He replied by telling the story of an old farmer who had a large shady tree towering over his house:

> It was a majestic-looking tree, and apparently perfect in every part, tall, straight, and of immense size, the grand old sentinel of his forest home. One morning, while at work in his garden, he saw a squirrel run up into a hole, which caused him to wonder whether the tree might be hollow. He decided to give it a thorough examination, and much to his disappointment, the stately tree he had prized for its beauty and grandeur and considered the pride and protection of his little farm, was actually hollow from top to bottom. Only a massive shell remained, barely sufficient to support its weight. What was he to do? If he cut it down, it would damage his home with its high and spreading branches. If he let it remain his family would be in constant danger. In a storm it might fall, or the wind might blow it down, and his house and children be crushed by it. What should he do?
>
> As he turned away, the farmer sighed sadly, 'I wish I had never set eyes on that squirrel!'

'Honest Abe', as President Lincoln was nicknamed, was not pretending to any quick or easy answers, but was telling his subordinate the truth. He admitted he was in a very real dilemma but was able to retain his reputation for integrity by accepting the truth though it was hard to hear.

Authority undermined by loss of integrity

Once a dog wandered into a preacher's home, and his sons played with it, fed it and soon became very fond of it. It so happened that the dog had three distinctive white hairs on its tail. One day, the preacher and his sons spotted an advertisement in the local newspaper about a lost dog. The description of the stray they had taken in exactly matched the one they had read about.

The minister later confessed, 'In the presence of my three sons, I carefully separated the three white hairs and removed them from the dog's tail.' The owner of the dog eventually discovered where his stray had gone and he came to claim him. The dog showed every sign of recognising his owner so the man was ready to take him away.

At that point the minister spoke up and asked, 'Didn't you say the dog would be known by three white hairs in its tail?' The owner, unable to find the identifying feature, was forced to admit that this dog didn't fully fit the description of his lost dog and left.

As the years passed the minister noted with sadness, 'We kept the dog but I lost my three sons for Christ that day.' The boys no longer had confidence in what their father professed to be true.

Integrity grows out of self-control

Self-control comes from a Greek word meaning 'strong', 'having mastery', 'able to control one's thought and actions'. John Wesley's mother once wrote to him while he was a student at Oxford that 'anything which increases the authority of the body over the mind is an evil thing'. Billy Graham reckoned that this comment has helped him to understand the meaning of self-control.

Diligence in small details

A famous architect Ludwig Mies van der Rohe once wrote significantly in the *New York Herald*, 'God is in the details'.

Leaders need to 'Sweat the small stuff'. (Rudolph Giuliani)

One of Judge Lumbard's rules was, 'Never assume a d*** thing.' In other words make sure you do your homework thoroughly.

Poem

I would be true, for there are those who trust me;
I would be pure, for there are those who care;
I would be strong for there are those who suffer;
I would be brave, for there is much to dare.
I would be friend of all – the foe and the friendless;
I would be giving, and forget the gift;
I would be humble, for I know my weakness;
I would look up, and laugh, and love, and lift.

(Howard Walter)

Psalm
'A good man ... will guide his affairs with discretion' (Psalm 112:5 NKJV).

Prayer
If my soul has turned perversely to the dark;
If I have left some brother wounded by the way;
If I have preferred my aims to Thine;
If I have been impatient and would not wait
If I have marred the pattern drawn out for my life;
If I have cost tears to those I loved:
If my heart has mourned against Thy will,
    O Lord forgive. (F. B. Meyer)

CHAPTER 10

People who risk vulnerability

'Yet of myself I will not glory, but of mine infirmities.'
(2 CORINTHIANS 12:5)

'When I am weak then I am strong.'
(2 CORINTHIANS 12:10)

DON'T BE A FAKE!

Some may think it odd to highlight vulnerability after talking about integrity, but in fact they are the two sides of the same coin. Vulnerability is an essential part of our humanity. We were all born as 'fallen' creatures. We have all grown up with particular weaknesses. We all do battle with our old natures. We are all tempted to keep on sinning. Sadly, we often fall, while, by the grace of God we may increasingly overcome. To pretend otherwise is to deceive ourselves. We cannot, and must not, claim that we never fail or that we are invulnerable. If we do, we will quickly erect a barrier of unreality between ourselves and our followers. They will soon conclude that we are fakes.

Perhaps we feel it will undermine our authority if we show our wounds, reveal our weaknesses or admit our failures. But to do that is to hide our true humanity. Again we may imagine that if we disclose our vulnerability our followers will never fully trust us again! Obviously, it is unhealthy and unproductive for leaders to labour morbidly and publicly over their personal follies and private failures. But it helps others to know we are just as weak as they are when we make a point of including ourselves as needing God's grace, mercy and forgiveness, just like everyone else.

Identifying with people in this way will help them more easily identify with us. We are attracted to Jesus because of his tears, his wounds, his subjection to the same temptations that we undergo.

QUOTES

- There is something vulgar about success. The greatest fail or seem to have failed. (Oscar Wilde)
- You can't learn surgery in a comfortable office. (Comment to medical students)
- Leaders need a high threshold of pain. (Anon)
- It is good for a leader to say 'I don't know' when he knows he doesn't. (Anon)
- It's not great men who change the world, but weak men in the hands of a great God. (Brother Yun, *The Heavenly Man*)
- It is better to accept vulnerability than to crave admirability. (Anon)
- Do I allow anyone around me to tell me when I have no clothes on? (Anon)
- I discovered an astonishing truth: God is attracted to weakness. He can't resist those who humbly and honestly admit how desperately they need him. (Jim Cymbala, *Fresh Wind, Fresh Fire*)

ILLUSTRATIONS
The value of a scar

One day our eight-year-old son, Thane, came in from outside, agitated and aroused.

'Look at my skateboard,' he exclaimed. 'It's got a scar on it!'

'I'm sorry, Thane,' I replied with concern, 'maybe we can rub it out!'

'What do you mean Dad, why would you do that? I want scars on my skateboard!'

Sensing that I was about to learn something significant, I asked, 'What do skateboard scars mean to you, Thane?'

'A scar means you're getting better, Dad. So the more scars on your skateboard, the better you are. I know someone at school who had so many scars on his skateboard that it broke!' (Leonard Sweet)

It was said that when the Knights of King Arthur returned from battle, if his men did not bear in their bodies some fresh scar, they were thrust forth by the King with the command, 'Go, get your scar!'

Christ does not look for medals – he looks for scars.

People value a vulnerable leader

In 1873 Father Damian, a Belgian Catholic priest, was sent to minister to leprosy sufferers on the Hawaiian island of Molokai. He arrived in high spirits, hoping to build a friendship with each of them. However, at every turn, people shunned him. He built a chapel, began worship services, poured out his heart to those with the disease, but all seemed in vain, however hard he tried. No one responded to his ministry and after twelve years of struggling, Father Damien eventually decided to leave. There was nothing more that he could do. As he stood in dejection on the dock waiting to board, he looked down at his hands and noticed some mysterious white spots on them. Feeling some numbness, he knew immediately that he had contracted leprosy!

He decided to return to the leprosy colony and to his work. Word spread quickly and within hours, hundreds gathered outside his hut, fully identifying with his plight. A bigger surprise came the following Sunday when he arrived at the chapel, and he found it full.

Father Damien began to preach from the empathy of love rather than his professional obligation, and his ministry became enormously effective.

Hiding our vulnerability

The whole day long I hear nothing else but that I'm actually an insufferable baby, and although I laugh about it, and pretend not to take any notice, I do mind. I would like to ask God to give me a different nature so that I didn't put everyone's back up. But that can't be done. I've got the nature that has been given to me and I'm sure it can't be bad. I do my very best to please everybody, far more than they'd ever guess. I try to laugh it all off because I don't want to let them see my trouble. (Anna Frank)

Unwilling to risk his royal vulnerability

Christopher Columbus worked out a plan whereby he might reach the East by sailing West. He presented his project to King John of Portugal, who at that time was Spain's rival for the colonial supremacy of the whole earth. Tentatively the king agreed to sponsor the venture when he saw how it might make Portugal the greatest nation on earth, but his advisers told him he would be laughed at from one end of Europe to the other if he financed the project. So the disappointed Columbus left Portugal and went to Isabella, Queen of Spain. Her councillors, too, laughed at the idea but the Queen refused to be put off. She said she would even pawn her jewels if necessary to back the expedition. History tells us the rest - how Spain 'discovered' America.

HYMN

Guide me O thou great Jehovah
Pilgrim through this barren land;
I am weak but thou art mighty;
Hold me with they powerful hand.

(William Williams)

PRAYER

Dear God
I hold up my weakness to your strength,
My failure to your faithfulness,
My sinfulness to your perfection,
My loneliness to your compassion,
My small pain to your agony on the cross.

(An adaptation by a prisoner serving a life sentence)

CHAPTER 11

People who can discern mood and momentum

'Leadership is a matter of timing.'
(ROBERT WARREN)

*Who knoweth whether thou art come to the kingdom f
or such a time as this.*
(ESTHER 4:14)

*The children if Issachar were men that had understanding
of the times to know what Israel ought to do.*
(I CHRONICLES 12:32)

*'My time has **not yet come.'***
(JESUS – JOHN 7:6, EMPHASIS ADDED)

*'I have many things to say to you but **you can't bear them now.'***
(JESUS – JOHN 16:12, EMPHASIS ADDED)

*'A word **spoken in due season,** how good is it!'*
(PROVERBS 15:23B KJV, EMPHASIS ADDED)

*Children learn at an early age to wait until their parents are in a
good mood to hit them for 'whatever the market will bear'.*
(HARVEY MACKAY)

THE IMPORTANCE OF TIMING

Good leaders learn to wait for the right opportunity, for the appropriate moment. When leaders have chosen the wrong moment, this has led to disastrous consequences. Governments have sometimes released bad news under the cover of another major announcement, but the carefully planned ruse has misfired because the public mood had been misjudged. There are two words for time in Greek. One is *Chronos* and the other is *Kairos*. The former denotes the hours and minutes on the sundial (the clock face today), the latter conveys the idea of the right moment to strike. It is the latter we are thinking about.

The Israelites had failed to attack when God had commanded. Moses had warned them of God's displeasure. Realising they had behaved stupidly they then changed their minds. Completely on their own initiative they decided to enter the Promised Land without any reference to God.

> And they rose early in the morning and went up to the top of the mountain, saying, 'Here we are, and we will go up to the place which the LORD has promised, for we have sinned!' And Moses said, 'Now why do you transgress the command of the LORD? For this will not succeed. Do not go *up*, lest you be defeated by your enemies, for the LORD is not among you. For the Amalekites and the Canaanites are there before you, and you shall fall by the sword; because you have turned away from the LORD, the LORD will not be with you.' But they presumed to go up to the mountain-top.. Nevertheless ... the Amalekites and the Canaanites who dwelt in that mountain came down and attacked them, and drove them back ...
>
> (Numbers 14:40–45 NKJV, emphasis added)

At a later period in Israel's history David is told to wait and attack his enemies at the right time:

> Then the Philistines went up once again and deployed themselves in the Valley of Rephaim. Therefore David inquired of the LORD, and He said, 'You shall not go up; circle around behind them, and come upon them in front of the mulberry trees. And it shall be, when you hear the sound of marching in the tops of the mulberry trees, *then* you shall advance quickly.'
>
> (2 Samuel 5:22–24a NKJV, emphasis added)

There is a tide in the affairs of men,
Which taken at the flood, leads on to fortune;
Omitted, all the voyage of their life
Is bound in shallows and in miseries,
On such a full sea are we now afloat,
And we must take the current when it serves
Or lose our venture.

(Shakespeare, *Julius Caesar*)

Common responses to new ideas
- That's impossible.
- We don't do things that way around here. Its too radical for us.
- We tried something like that before and it didn't work.
- I wish it were that easy.
- It's against our policy to do it that way.
- When you've been around a little longer, you'll understand.
- Who gave you the permission to change the rules?
- Let's get real, OK?
- How dare you suggest that what we are doing is wrong?
- If you had been in this field as long as I have, you would understand that what you are suggesting is absolutely absurd!

Situation sensing!
Sven-Goran Eriksson's successful management style of England's football team is credited with a major 'soft' skill described as 'situation sensing', an awareness of what the situation really is and being able to adapt to it accordingly. 'Great leaders are very adept at sensing the atmosphere in their organisation. They can sniff out the signals in the environment and sense what's going on without having it spelled out for them' (Rob Goffee). The importance of understanding moods at the different levels of an organisation, and developing ways to lift spirits or lighten the atmosphere in an appropriate manner is a major asset. Leaders also need to understand the significance of momentum. As Lee Iacocca has said 'Even the right decision is wrong if it's made too late.' Or if it is announced when the mood and momentum are clearly against it.

Too soon and too sudden

Too many disasters have resulted from young leaders who wanted to make their mark by launching a plan or changing direction too soon or too suddenly. When a large liner has been travelling at speed for some time it is difficult to change direction without slowing down almost to a standstill. It will be doubly hard to gather momentum again following such a body shock to the systems of a church.

QUOTES

- Leaders need to choose what to measure in life – the real booby trap is to measure the wrong thing. (Max DePree)
- If the ladder is against the wrong wall then every step we take gets us to the wrong place. (Betty Maltz)
- A good leader can sense when the Holy Spirit of God is moving. (Anon)
- A good leader is aware of the human spirit's responses in other people. (Anon)
- Short-term results are not the same as long-term needs. (Max DePree)
- Leaders recognise and appreciate both the essential contribution and limitation of their team members. (Anon)
- The real danger is blind complacency. (Max DePree)
- Not to see our choices may be worse than making poor decisions. (Anon)
- The key to success lies in the way we exploit our freedom, make our choices and anticipate consequences. (Max DePree)
- The true leader knows how to prioritise. (Anon)
- Max did everything by feel – you could not have a detailed argument with him. (Press Comment about Max Hastings, war historian and one-time editor of the *Daily Telegraph*)
- Jesus has not given us detailed instructions on how to handle every situation. (Bill Hybels)
- The first step to wisdom is to listen; the second is silence. (Anon)
- We don't know what the future holds, but we know who holds the future. (Billy Graham)

- Leaders must sense needs and feelings of colleagues, congregations and organisations. (Anon)
- Understanding that the way citizens would perceive the information they were getting was as important as the information itself. (Rudoph Giuliani – ex-mayor of New York City)
- The door to the room of success swings on the hinges of opportunity. (Anon)
- Consultation is required in any model of leadership. (Mike Brearley)
- The hallmark of a great captain is the ability to win the toss at the right time. (Richie Bernaud, Australian cricketer and commentator)
- The more people you lead, the more you must listen. (Hanz Finzel)

ILLUSTRATIONS
Three leadership attributes
Sven-Goran Eriksson appears to possess three key attributes that operate effectively in his leadership style.
1. Situation sensing
2. Authenticity – he is true to himself
3. Empathy – he knows how to identify with others and see the world through their eyes.

Evaluating what counts
Jeff Ostrander writes of an old man on the east coast of North America, who went down to the beach alone every day. As the tide was receding he would walk for miles along the sandy shore.

A neighbour observed that, as he walked, he would often stoop to pick up something from the wet sand and pitch it back into the vast Atlantic. Dying with curiosity, the neighbour decided to find out exactly what he was doing and observed that the old man was picking up starfish that had been stranded by the retreating tide and throwing them back into the sea. They would, of course, normally die of dehydration before the next tide came in. Calling out to him the neighbour said, 'Hey, what do you think you are doing? Thousands of starfish get stranded on this beach every day! Do you really think that throwing a few back is going to matter?'

The old man paused for a moment listening, then he held out a starfish toward his neighbour and said, 'It matters to this one.'

Missing the mood

The head of BBC Religious Broadcasting in the seventies once tried to reinstate what might be called the true calendar of Christmas. He directed the department that no carols should be played over the air until after the last Sunday in Advent, and then to continue playing them until Epiphany (6 January). This resulted in squeals of protests from churches and choirs, not to mention the listening public.

Meanwhile the disc jockeys were in full run-up-to-Christmas mode, including jazzed-up versions of carols, and some proper ones, and the rest of the BBC got stuck into the festive air with its customary over-indulgence. But when the religious department finally got around to including carols in services, further protests erupted: 'Why are you still playing carols? We've had enough of them. Christmas is over, hadn't you noticed?'[1]

Crisis leadership

The word 'crisis' in Chinese is composed of two characters. One represents danger and the other represents *opportunity*. (Gerald Horton Bath)

Biblical quote

'And a wise man's heart discerns both time and judgment,
Because for every matter there is a time and judgment.'
(Ecclesiastes 8:5b,6a NKJV)

Parody of Prayer

Grant me the ability
To forget the people
I never liked anyway,
The good fortune to meet
the ones I always liked
And the discernment
To tell the difference.

Prayer

Lord give me a right spirit to discern the voice of God; to discern the hand of God; to discern the times of God; to discern the judgements of God; to discern the men and women of God; to discern the potential in the church of God; to discern the priorities of the Kingdom of God and finally, to discern the true motives of my own heart. For Christ's sake. Amen.

CHAPTER 12

People who can delegate and work as a team

One of the major problems a pastor ... faces is the issue of role change in a growing church.

(JOHN WIMBER)

We use the word 'delegate' with caution. Many of today's generation understand it as 'the language of control'. Apparently we need to learn 'the language of empowerment'.

(EDDIE GIBBS)

Leaders of growing churches concentrate on the empowering of other Christians for ministry.

(CHRISTIAN A. SCHWARZ)

In this world it is not what we take up, but what we give up, that makes us rich.

(HENRY WARD BEECHER)

BALANCE WEAKNESSES WITH THE STRENGTHS OF OTHERS

Rudolph Giuliani, ex-mayor of New York, who led the city through the tragic aftermath of the 9/11 World Trade Center attacks, dedicated his book *Leadership* to 'all the people ... whom I leaned upon and learned from'. He goes on to say, 'Looking back, I believe that the skill I developed better than any other was surrounding myself with great people ... the goal is to balance your weaknesses with the strengths of others.'

Significant leaders have to acknowledge that they owe so much of their 'success' to the good people around them. Some of this help comes from spontaneous gifted amateurs who are available at the opportune moments of crises, and much of it from those to whom it has been prayerfully and thoughtfully delegated. Rudolph Giuliani further comments, 'I can barely describe what it meant to me to know that I could turn something over to someone and know that it would get done, without having to hector or to micromanage.'

It's worth mentioning here the value of surrounding oneself with leaders who feel free to disagree. 'A king with chieftains who always agree with him, reaps the counsel of mediocrity.' (Attila the Hun)

From delegation back to centralisation

Adolf Hitler initially was very successful because he adopted a mission command, whereby he shared his overall aim with his officers but allowed them to make the tactical decisions on the battlefield. Later on he began to mistrust officers when he heard that they were critical of his merciless brutality, and he reverted to central command. It is significant that it was from that point on that he began to lose the war on every front. Good leaders delegate to their subordinates, and trust them.

Spelling out what delegation means

Delegation consists in transferring authority, responsibility, and accountability from one person or group to another. In most cases, it involves moving authority from a higher level in an organisation to a lower one. Delegation is the process by which decentralisation of organisational power occurs. (Myron Rush, *Management: A Biblical Approach*)

Authority represents the decision-making power needed to achieve the assigned responsibility.

Responsibility ensures that the person to whom a task is delegated understands exactly what has to be done and to whom s/he is accountable.

Accountability is the obligation to perform one's responsibility and the exercise of one's authority under the terms, and according to the standards, laid down by the leader or any higher authority.

Delegation needs a job description

Besides taking time with those to whom one delegates, it is important to give the person a written job description with a review after three months, and a built-in time limit, say a year or two, to complete the task. The time can always be extended later but without the limit it is difficult to remove people if they are causing problems or not doing too well, while others are available who could do the job better or fit in more happily.

Guidelines to clear delegation

1. Spend time praying it over.
2. Consult others.
3. Select qualified people.
4. Show you trust them.
5. Clarify their duties.
6. Give them the appropriate authority.
7. Do not tell them how to do the work.
8. Ensure times along the way for accountability.
9. Give them room to fail occasionally.
10. Give them praise and credit for work well done. (Anon)

Classic example

The classic example of delegation is found in the book of Exodus where Jethro counsels his son-in-law Moses:

And so it was, on the next day, that Moses sat to judge the people; and the people stood before Moses from morning until evening. So when Moses' father-in-law saw all that he did for the people, he said, 'What is this thing that you are doing for the people? Why do you alone sit, and all the people stand before you from morning until evening?'

And Moses said to his father-in-law, 'Because the people come to me to inquire of God. When they have a difficulty, they come to me, and I judge between one and another; and I make known the statutes of God and His laws.'

So Moses' father-in-law said to him, 'The thing that you do is not good. Both you and these people who are with you will surely wear yourselves out. For this thing is too much for you; you are not able to perform it by yourself. Listen now to my voice; I will give you counsel, and God will be with you: Stand before God for the people, so that you may bring the difficulties to God. And you shall teach them the statutes and the laws, and show them the way in which they must walk and the work they must do. Moreover you shall select from all the people able men, such as fear God, men of truth, hating covetousness; and place such over them to be rulers of thousands, rulers of hundreds, rulers of fifties, and rulers of tens. And let them judge the people at all times. Then it will be that every great matter they shall bring to you, but every small matter they themselves shall judge. So it will be easier for you, for they will bear the burden with you. If you do this thing, and God so commands you, then you will be able to endure, and all this people will also go to their place in peace.' So Moses heeded the voice of his father-in-law and did all that he had said. And Moses chose able men out of all Israel, and made them heads over the people: rulers of thousands, rulers of hundreds, rulers of fifties, and rulers of tens. So they judged the people at all times; the hard cases they brought to Moses, but they judged every small case themselves.

(Exodus 18:13–26 NKJV)

Delegation never means abdication

All effective leaders learn to delegate, but delegating leadership authority to others does not imply abdication. The 'top person' must still 'own' the work delegated by keeping a constant interest in it, by supporting and encouraging it. From the start it must be made quite clear to the person taking delegated authority that s/he is accountable to the leader.

If this is not done the house may well find that it is divided against itself. President Truman avoided such a crisis when he placed a boldly printed card on his desk for all to see. It read, 'The Buck Stops Here.'

Delegation is a trust

If one is delegating to the right person (and it is not a good idea to delegate to the wrong person!) then one can trust him/her to get on with the job. The leader needs to keep close enough to encourage but not to control or meddle. General George Paton once said: 'Never tell people how to do things. Tell them what to do and they will surprise you with their ingenuity.' Proffer your wisdom if requested, but do not push it. Responsible people may not follow office hours exactly but they will not usually abuse their freedom. If you have any bones to pick then pick the most significant ones, but only after you have prayed about it and made a point of first giving credit and encouragement for any positive achievements and reports so far.

Delegation is a risk

Delegating is risk-taking. Jesus Christ prayed through the night before appointing the twelve apostles – and even one of them betrayed him. Delegators need the ability to recognise ability. It was said of W. E. Sangster, once a leader within the Methodist Church in Britain, that 'perhaps his greatest grasp of leadership was knowing the importance of delegation and of choosing assistants'. J. Oswald Sanders, a missionary statesman, once wrote, 'One definition of leadership is the ability to recognise the special abilities and limitations of others, combined with the capacity to fit each one into the job where he will do his best.'

Delegation is a release

- Delegation releases the leader to fulfil his primary responsibilities in the church.
- Delegation increases the amount of work that gets done and allows a church to develop to its full potential. The captain does not have to score the goals but to ensure that winning goals are scored.
- Delegation will save the leader from burnout or breakdown from over-work.
- Delegation is the most practical way of training others.
- Delegate only to people who are loyal to you as leader and loyal to the organisation. Never mistake loyalty for 'yes men'.
- Delegate only to people who will do the job well. Do not delegate to people who would love to do the job for emotional reasons or who desire a position, without evidence that they would do the job effectively. Appointing unsatisfactory people sooner or later creates a greater set of problems for both the leader and the church. Look for people who will be good at solving your problems, not those liable to create more problems for you.

Delegating is a sacrifice

It is relatively easy to give away areas of work in which we are weak, but harder to give away areas in which we think we do rather well, and especially those areas we have really enjoyed doing.

Some small church leaders may not fully understand the cost involved in delegation. Often there is serious misunderstanding from within the church itself. When the church was small the pastor may well 'have had an "open door" policy in which people were encouraged to "drop in"... After church growth the pastor has to change to an "appointment only" policy because of the demands on time. People who have always been able to "get in" now can't and are often angered by it.' (John Wimber)

Leaders need not be inhibited about delegating to others things they dislike doing, on the assumption that others won't like doing it either. People like doing what they like doing, and leaders may be surprised to find that there will always be people around who really like doing things others dislike having to do.

Delegation to remove a threat
An insecure leader may well feel threatened by the love and praise being piled on an assistant. When I was serving in Latin America it was said that Fidel Castro made a point of getting his popular associate, Che Guevara, posted to Cuban missions abroad. Certainly Stalin made a point of removing any hero-worshipped generals from the limelight when they came home from the war.

'One need not feel threatened by capable contemporaries or subordinates. Be wise in selecting capable captains to achieve those things a chieftain can only attain through strong subordinates.' (King Attila the Hun)

QUOTES
- Delegation is a way of dealing with the increasing complexity in an organisation. (Anon)
- While good delegation is a form of dying, it is in fact the only way for leaders to stay alive ... but delegate poorly and the leader will die a thousand deaths. (Anon)
- We must surrender or abandon ourselves to the gifts that others bring to the game. (Max DePree)
- We become effective operators by trusting that others can do some things better than we can. (Max DePree)

- Trust is the network of our interdependence. (Anon)
- It is only as we develop others that we permanently succeed. (Harvey S. Firstone)
- By delegating to others, leaders give roots, and they also give wings. (Anon)
- Delegation must never mean abdication. (Anon)
- Today's leader gets things done through other people. (Anon)
- We believe in the power of we, not me. (Home Shopping Network, Florida)
- Before making any proposal formally, let your team work over it privately and make it as acceptable as possible to all concerned. (David Pytches)
- Surround yourself with great people. (Rudolph Giuliani – cf his book *Leadership*)
- The one who gets the job should decide how it is done. (Hans Finzel)
- Delegation should match each worker's follow-through ability. (Hans Finzel)
- Part of good leadership is giving others under your authority the same tools you'd expect [yourself]. (Rudolph Giuliani)
- Here lies a man who attracted better people into his service than he was himself. (Andrew Carnegie's expressed wish for his epitaph)

ILLUSTRATIONS
Motive to be worthy
One of my greatest resources these ten years in Poland is the sense of his [Dr John Mott's] backing. My greatest pride is his belief in me. Surely one of the greatest motives is to be worthy of his support and to measure up to his expectation of me.[1]

Warning to be careful
I once read a news item that I felt God showed me was a parable

A Chinese cook was preparing a meal of snakes. He cut off their heads, skinned the bodies and prepared the dish. He then cleaned up and in the process scooped up the heads in his hands to dispose of them in the garbage. In doing so, apparently one of the snakes' heads bit him, resulting tragically in his death.

Great care has to be taken about removing leaders: there can be unforeseen consequences and it should never be rushed into. It might be wise to find some other tasks involving a sideways move, as a damage-limitation exercise.

Be careful not to give positions important sounding titles. It appeals to the wrong motives. Jesus constantly stressed the servant nature of leadership.

Beware the pessimists

If you surround yourself with pessimists you're doomed to failure in business. They are the voices you can't let in your head. If you listen to the pessimists you'll make the wrong decision or be so confused and so befuddled you'll lose the emotional energy you need. (James R. Cramer, Cramer, Berkowitz & Company)

Building for success

The explorer, Sir Ernest Shackleton, built success on a foundation of camaraderie, loyalty, responsibility, determination and, above all, optimism. (Margot Morrell and Stephanie Capparell)

The archetypal team leader today

Sven-Goran Eriksson, the Swede who coaches for England, stresses the importance of teamwork and co-operation, the ability to create consensus and commitment around a vision, and a preference for direct dialogue with team members.[2] This is a style that is inherently fragile but it makes a leader someone others will want to rally around.

VERSE

Give me men to match my mountains,
Bring me men to match my plains,
Men with empires in their purpose
And new eras in their brains.

(Sam Foss, from an early history of California)

BIBLICAL QUOTE

'Without counsel, plans go awry,
But in the multitude of counsellors
they are established'
                    (Proverbs 15:22 NKJV).

PRAYER

Lord, I know it's silly to think of doing this job on my own, but if I am going to ask others to help me I need to ask the right ones, and so I need your help because you know what is in all of us and you have good plans for everyone: so please guide me to the right people by your Holy Spirit. For Christ's sake. Amen.

CHAPTER 13

People who make careful decisions and take courageous moves

'Be strong and of a good courage.'

(JOSHUA 1:6 KJV)

'Only be strong and very courageous.'

(JOSHUA 1:7 NKJV)

'Have not I commanded thee? Be strong and of a good courage.'

(JOSHUA 1:9 KJV)

I can now see, looking back, that every significant step forward in the life of the church has involved risk.

(ROBERT WARREN)

NO HEAD FOR HEIGHTS

I once asked a life-long school master, and obviously a good one, why he retired from a headship after only a short period of time. He said that when he was younger he fully expected he would naturally move into such a position one day. But when it came to it, he told me, there were two reasons why he was uncomfortable in the job, one was that he was too soft skinned and the other that he found decision-making too difficult – an honest self-assessment which probably saved him from breaking down and the school from breaking up.

LEADERS ARE OBLIGED TO MAKE DECISIONS

Leadership is about making decisions. Life is about making choices and church life is the same. A leader cannot be tentative. There can be no 'nailing of colours to the fence'! Leaders are expected to make decisions. When a decision needs to be made but is not taken, doing nothing is taken as the leader's decision. Winston Churchill used to say of a certain Prime Minister that 'If you want nothing done, [then he, the Prime Minister], was the best man for the task. There is none equal to him.' Apparently this particular PM was averse to making any decisions and left his cabinet members frantic with frustration.

Some people just don't seem to be able to make decisions, especially if there is a possibility of provoking opposition or the probability of hurting someone's feelings. And some good people, like the headmaster cited above, are just not cut out for that particular role.

But those who are called to leadership must learn, after due consideration, to make decisions wisely, humbly and lovingly. Nothing is more exasperating than having to work for a dithering leader. One bishop once boasted that he always looked to see which way things were moving before he then took up a position at their head! Making a lot of decisions does not necessarily raise morale, but failure to take decisions almost certainly lowers it.

LEADERS ARE CALLED TO TAKE RISKS

One thing that historians identify about great leaders is their ability to make courageous moves, leading to victory in battle.

One can think of a long list of John Bunyan's fellow pilgrims, Christian saints along the way, who would never have made leaders for others to follow – Mr Fearing, Mr Feeble-mind, Mr Ready-to-Halt, Mr Despondency and his daughter, Much Afraid. They all kept struggling on as though tormented by the grisly feeling that they would never make it. Such would not inspire hope in others by their feats of courage, though by the grace of God they would eventually reach the heavenly city.

The people who most inspired me were men who boldly confronted danger – Allen Gardiner, who died of starvation on a deserted cove in Tierra del Fuego; John G. Paton, who gave long years to mission among the cannibals in the New Hebrides; or Jim Elliot who gave his life as a martyr for the fierce Aucas in the darkest forests of Ecuador. Those were my heroes. Leaders do not have to make many life-threatening choices but every now and again courageous moves will have to be made.

Cowards die many times before their deaths;
The valiant never taste of death but once.
(Shakespeare, Julius Caesar)

QUOTES

- It's the start that stops most people. (Anon)
- Only those who risk going too far can possibly find out how far one can go. (T. S. Elliot)
- Don't go where the path may be. Go instead where there is no path, and leave a trail. (Ralph Waldo Emerson)
- Her great strength was to challenge the conventional wisdom. (Lord Charles Powell talking about Baroness Thatcher as a Prime Minister, BBC 2, 22 March 2002)
- The best run schools are being led by grey-haired revolutionaries with 'an almost complete indifference to externally imposed agendas'. (Anon)
- They [the most successful school heads] tended to possess a towering self-confidence and the courage to break through traditional and institutional thinking, and relationships, to pursue different agendas. (Anon)
- True leadership requires choosing ... the position that allows you to sleep at night. (Rudolph Guiliani)
- When the going gets tough, the tough get going. (Anon)
- You miss 100 per cent of the shots you never take. (Wayne Gretzky, Canadian ice hockey hero)
- Often risks that look like folly turn out to be the wisdom of God. (Christopher Cocksworth)
- Safety is for wimps. Safety is for losers. (Christopher Cocksworth)
- People will sometimes forgive you for making bad decisions as long as you are willing to make decisions. (Max Hastings)
- I am immortal until my work is done. (John Wesley)
- Anyone can steer the ship but it takes a leader to chart the course. (John C. Maxwell)
- Procrastination becomes a state of mind and filters through

the whole organisation. (Rudolph Giuliani)
- Not to make a decision is a decision in itself – plenty of action can happen through inaction. (Eddy Gibbs)
- What a shame – yes, how stupid! – to decide before knowing the facts! (Proverbs 18:13 Living Bible)
- A leader must not let critics set the agenda. (Rudolph Giuliani)
- Often I make a decision knowing I'll be criticised, but feeling certain that I'll be vindicated. (Rudolph Giuliani)
- Never make a serious decision when you are feeling tired or ill. (Advice given to Billy Graham)
- Nothing is so exhausting as indecision and nothing is so futile. (Bertrand Russell)
- There will always be those who are frightened by boldness and cowed by the necessity of making decisions. (F. D. Roosevelt, *Fireside Chat* 1934)
- Leadership is the ability to hide your panic from others. (Anon)
- Nothing succeeds in war like a good plan. (Napoleon Bonaparte)
- Make decisions with your head not your heart. Making them with the heart terminates with heart disease. (Harvey Mackay)
- Courage is fear that has said its prayers. (Karle Wilson Baker)
- He nailed his colours firmly to the fence. (Garreth Bennett)
- Decisions can take you out of God's will but never out of his reach. (Anon)
- Courage is that quality of mind which enables men to encounter danger or difficulty with firmness, or without fear or depression of spirits … The highest degree of courage is seen in the person who is most fearful but refuses to capitulate to it. (J. Oswald Sanders)
- We need to spend money on research and development before we can be sure of the way ahead. (Robert Warren)
- The hottest fires in Hell are reserved for those who, in a period of moral crisis, maintain their neutrality. (Dante)
- An early-20th century missionary going to China was asked, 'Aren't you afraid?' She replied, 'I am afraid of only one thing

– that I will become a grain of wheat unwilling to die.'

ILLUSTRATIONS
Decisions are imperative for progress
Business executives know that it is sometimes difficult to implement decisions that have major impact on an organisation. Willingness to make decisions is not easy to come by ... but decisions must be made ... Consider for a moment what a company is like *without* effective decisiveness. Nothing happens and opportunities are lost. People wander about aimlessly, aggressive employees become frustrated, and lethargic employees are not motivated. But in a corporation *with* decisive leaders the atmosphere is dynamic and vibrant. People move with a spring in their step and purpose in their direction ... Competent executive decision-making is crucial in any organisation. (Donald Phillips)

Disinclination for risk taking
J.C. Penney, who worked as a sales clerk in a department store in his early years was inspired by his supervisor's dream of one day running his own store.

Some twenty-five years later, after starting his own J. C. Penney Company with superstores across the country, Penney returned to the original store where he received his early training. He was greatly surprised to find his former supervisor still working there. When Penney asked him why he had never had a store of his own, he replied, 'Oh, too much risk. Here I have a decent job with good security, but if I had launched out with my own store I might have gone broke!'

Too many of us settle for failure by making the same mistake, never quite sure why. If we always do what we have always done, we will always get what we always got!

Difficulty in risk taking
The difficulty ... 'about risk-taking is that every time the church grows we seem to sense God's call to another step of faith. Yet each time the risk is bigger; the stakes become higher. However these events are points of growth and learning for the whole church. Indeed without the risks having been taken there would be little or no story to tell. Along the way I have learned something about faith

which has surprised me. Initially I had thought that faith was the absolute certainty which enables us to take the risk out of living. I now understand it to be God's gift which enables us to enter into risks with no certainty about the outcome other than that we will find God faithful.[1] (Robert Warren)

Decisions need to be good decisions

Making the right choices is the most important part of leadership. Every other element, from developing and communicating ideas, to surrounding oneself with great people, depends upon making good decisions. And the making of quick decisions in the times of crisis is often the hardest. Your decisions have to be based on arguments that are most convincing, allegiances that are most important to you and the well-being, development and advance of your community, congregation.

A business leader was once asked the secret of his success. He said it was the result of making right decisions!

'But how does one set about making the right decisions?' asked his younger friend.

'Experience,' came the reply.

'But how does one gain that experience?' the young man pressed him.

'By making wrong decisions!' replied the businessman.

Decisions need to be at the right time

One of the trickiest elements of decision-making is working out not what, but when. Regardless of how much time exists before a decision must be made, I never make up my mind until I have to.

Faced with any important decision, I always envision how each alternative will play out before I make it. During this process, I'm not afraid to change my mind a few times. Many are tempted to decide an issue simply to end the discomfort of indecision. However, the longer you have to make a decision, the more mature and well reasoned that decision should be. (Rudolph Giuliani)

Decision times needs discerning

John Scullery, when discussing his decision-making processes at Apple Computers said,

It's very intuitive. Just like a sailor can sniff the air and knows when a storm is coming up, I have always been good at sniffing the air and knowing when the time is right to change a course or direction or when to make a big investment.

In order to get his way on the timing of his D–Day landing for the invasion of Europe in the Second World War, Eisenhower compromised on non-essentials and also biding his time with the constant chafing of General Montgomery.[2]

Decisions must not be ducked

In a recent interview with the 69-year-old Australian comedian Barry Humphries, probably most famous for his portrayal of Dame Edna Everage, it emerged that he was into his fourth marriage, had suffered from serious drink problems with two spells in a psychiatric hospital, and admitted that he was happiest when he was at the airport with a boarding card in his breast pocket. He confessed that this could be due to the fact that 'staying in one place one is confronted with too many worrying and challenging things'. (*Sunday Telegraph Review* 28 December 2003)

Decisions demand wisdom

It was said of Major General Ambrose Everett Burnside that 'No advantage, numerical or tactical was so great that this general could not throw it away.' At the Battle of Antietam, during the American Civil War, Burnside overcame his advantage in having 12,000 men at his disposal, by ordering them to march single file across an exposed bridge on which numerous enemy guns were trained to pick them off one by one. Only later did he discover that the river was only waist deep and could have been forded without danger at any point.

A couple of years later Burnside ordered the dynamiting of a trench along which his men could safely reach the centre of the enemy camp. The smoke was still rising as his soldiers suddenly found there was now no way through. When the smoke had cleared their enemy discovered they had the whole force trapped in front of them in a six-foot trench. When this was reported to President Lincoln he wryly remarked, 'Only Burnside could have managed such a coup, wringing one last spectacular defeat from the very jaws of victory.'

Decisions demand energy

Years ago, the story goes, a hungry tramp begged a farmer to give him a job so that he could earn some quick money. The farmer took him to a barn and pointed out a huge pile of recently lifted potatoes. 'I need you to sort out these potatoes into big and small ones before I take them to market next week. There's enough work going here to keep you going for several days.'

The tramp settled down to his work, putting all the big potatoes into one pile and all the little ones in another. An hour later the farmer spotted the tramp slinking off to the road again.

'Where are you going?' called the farmer.

'I'm leaving,' said the tramp. 'Having to make so many decisions is driving me crazy!' (Anon)

Decisions demand courage

I once met a tank commander who had won the Victoria Cross for bravery as a young man. Full of admiration, and dying of curiosity, I asked him to tell me how he had done it, how he had found the courage. Servicemen were always reticent about 'swinging the lamp' – discussing what they did in the war – but I finally managed to persuade him.

He explained that his troops were on the front line in World War II. His job was to give them cover under the firepower from his tank. He said he had not felt in the slightest bit courageous at the time as he faced intense shelling from the enemy. He just knew quite simply that both his senior officer and the troops were relying on him to hold his position even though he was himself in a very vulnerable place.

Courage is resistance to fear, not the absence of it. Lack of courage does not excuse us from the call of God or the call of duty.

Decisions demand research

One of the great Christian social reformers of the 19th century was Sir Ashley Cooper, later Lord Shaftesbury. He had been converted to Christ through the family housekeeper, Maria Milles. One of the many reforms that he spearheaded concerned the dreadful conditions and long hours for women and children in the work places of his day.

Sir Ashley chaired a Royal Commission on the conditions of employment of children. He visited countless mills and factories, bad and good, met children crippled at work (discovering 'a whole alphabet' of deformities), and made a thorough study of the little known facts.

Unpopular findings

The findings made Sir Ashley extremely unpopular with industrialists. But, on 7 May 1842, Members of Parliament, and later the public, were shocked and disgusted by the thoroughly researched report which lay on their breakfast tables. So appalling were their discoveries that the Home Office tried to prevent publication of the Commissioner's report but 'It came,' said Ashley, 'by a most providential mistake, into the hands of Members.'

The text was illustrated by on-the-spot drawings, and men who had hitherto dismissed Ashley as a crank found their stomachs turning as they studied the pages. Enormities, which they fondly believed unthinkable in England, were being perpetuated underground, invisible to the general public, in the mines that belonged to noble lords and cultured men in leading fashionable circles.

Girls, almost naked and chained to heavy carts, were found drawing coals up low, narrow passages far underground; girls were having to work alongside naked men, who sometimes sexually abused them. Children of five, or even younger incarcerated without light, to work trapdoors in the rat-infested mines; children standing all day ankle-deep in water at the pumps. They were working twelve to fourteen hours a day, six days a week. Sometimes children were kept underground night and day. Brutal overseers continually used a strap or even pick-handles to punish and oppress.

'My boy, ten years old,' one woman swore on oath, 'was at work; his toe was cut off …; notwithstanding this, the loader made him work until the end of the day, although in great pain.'

Impact and reactions

The impact of this report was enormous. The conscience of the nation was aroused. Ashley put down a motion to introduce a Colliery Bill releasing children and women from slavery in the mines. Peel's Government tried to edge him out.

'No assistance, no sympathy,' Ashley wrote of them, '[putting] every obstacle in my way, though I doubt whether they will dare openly to oppose me on the Bill itself ... God, go before us, as in the pillar of cloud.'

On the day allotted for his Bill, Ashley was tricked into giving way to another matter. 'Never did I pass such an evening, expecting, for six hours, without food or drink, to be called on at any moment – very unwell in consequence.'

At last, a month after the publication of the report, Ashley rose in the House of Commons to introduce his Bill. The House was packed. 'As I stood at the table, and just before I opened my mouth, the words of God came forcibly to my mind, "Only be strong and of good courage ..."'

In deepening silence the House listened, as Sir Ashley disclosed what was happening to children and women down the mines. Some members wept. At the end of a tremendous speech he sat down to tumultuous cheering and the Bill was passed with commendable speed. By early August 1842 it became law.[3]

Decisions demand planning
Abraham Lincoln (President of the Northern Confederacy during North America's Civil War) had the will and the ability to make tough decisions when necessary. And he did not hesitate once he was convinced that swift action was called for.

However it is certain that for every crucial decision of his administration Lincoln thought things out well in advance. In fact, he employed a classic decision-making sequence of events that began with an understanding of all the facts that were involved, often obtaining this information himself by venturing into the [battle] field. Lincoln would also consider a variety of possible solutions and the consequences of each. Finally, he would assure himself that any social action taken would be consistent with his administrative and personal policy objectives. And then he would effectively communicate his decision and implement it. (Donald T. Phillips, *Lincoln on Leadership*)

Decision is determined by duty to God
The singular action of a sanctified Christian is to prefer the duty he owes to God to the danger he fears from man. Christians in all ages have prized their services above their safety. 'The wicked flee when no man pursueth: but the righteous are bold as a lion.' (William

Secker)

Decisions develop character

He [Ernest Shackleton] was essentially a fighter, afraid of nothing and of nobody, but, withal he was human, overflowing with kindness and generosity, affectionate and loyal to all his friends.[4] (Louis C. Bernacchi)

BIBLE VERSES

'If we are faithless, he will remain faithful, for he cannot disown himself.' (2 Timothy 2:13 NIV)

'Be strong and of good courage ... only be strong and very courageous' (God's word to Joshua, Israel's new leader.. Joshua 1:6,7, 9,18)

PRAYER

Lord, you have promised that your Holy Spirit will guide your servants and I need your directions now as I travel through shadows in the valley of decision. In your light we see light, so please shine a light on my path to show me your will today. Let me hear that voice behind me telling me which way to go. Then Lord when that seems clear, give me the courage to call others to follow, and the patience to endure their faltering doubts. For the sake of your kingdom and the glory of Jesus. Amen.

CHAPTER 14

People with a good sense of humour

'A merry heart maketh a cheerful countenance.'
(PROVERBS 15:13 KJV)

'He that is of a merry heart hath a continual feast.'
(PROVERBS 15:15 KJV)

LAUGHTER THERAPY
Some things in life should be done for the pure fun of it, just for a good wholesome belly laugh. People feel better after laughing, both physically and emotionally.

When Norman Cousins was told that he had a virtually incurable disease that would finally claim his life (due to a serious deterioration of the spinal cord), he decided to have as many humorous and hilarious films brought to his hospital room as his family could lay hands on. Daily he watched re-runs of comedy shows such as the *Three Stooges, Abbott and Costello*, etc. You might call this 'laughter therapy' but it really effected wonderful results for him. His best-selling true story, *Anatomy of an Illness*, told how he was cured of his terminal illness through the medicine of laughter.

CHANGING THE CHEMISTRY
When humans laugh, we literally change the chemistry of our bodies. Peptides and endorphins are introduced into our bloodstream through smiling and laughing, and these can have an enormous healing impact on the body. Tears caused by laughter even have a different chemical makeup from tears caused by sorrow and sadness.

Dr Patrick Dixon, in his book *Signs of Revival*, discusses the positive role of emotions. He explains, for example, how the actual mechanism of laughing affects the whole body. Laughter helps the lungs, refreshes the brain, and sometimes eases muscle tension in cases of neuralgia and rheumatism.

> It alters the levels of various 'stress' hormones and growth hormones – all released when we are tense, working hard, worried or afraid … On the other hand we can develop stomach ulcers, arteries can clog up, we may become irritable and develop a host of other problems – all because the body is pumping out hormones we don't need. Laughter inhibits these hormone levels, and keeps them low … it helps to prevent some of the damage that stress causes us. Not surprisingly it makes us feel more relaxed.

PERSONAL EXPERIENCE

I have often found how a humorous aside can clear the air in a council meeting, or break the tension when confronted with a seemingly insurmountable difference of opinion. I was intrigued recently to discover that Mayor Rudolph Giuliani would typically begin the daily meetings of his high-powered staff 'with a few minutes of joking around'. He believed that this simple practice of daily joking helped to prevent resentments from festering.

It is interesting to note that in Norway today managers are being sent on *smilekurses* where they learn how to laugh and smile better, and therefore the reasoning goes, to serve better. Of course, as Christians we must always take God very seriously indeed, and there are many things that happen in our world that make us want to weep, but it's unwise usually to take ourselves too seriously. After all, people do some very funny things and we can either laugh or cry about them, to balance up with the times where laughing would be quite inappropriate. 'There are times to weep and times to laugh; times to mourn and times to dance.' (Ecclesiastes 3:4)

QUOTES

- 'A merry heart doeth good like a medicine' (Proverbs 17:22 KJV)
- Humour is a very funny thing. (Terry Johnson, *Dead Funny Play*)
- [Comedy is] the kindly contemplation of the incongruous. (P. G. Wodehouse)

- Laughter is a tranquillizer with no harmful side effects. (Anon)
- Comedy is medicine. (Trevor Griffiths)
- Humour is proof of good faith. (Charles M. Schulz)
- Laughter is holy. (Canon Edwyn Davies)
- A joke is a very serious thing. (Charles Churchill)
- I look for something slightly quirky, maybe a quotation or something that shows a sense of humour.[1] (Dr Brenda Cross)
- It's an odd job making decent people laugh. (Moliere)
- His foe was folly and his weapon wit. (Inscription on the Victoria Embankment tablet to W. S. Gilbert)
- Freedom produces jokes and jokes produce freedom. (Jean Paul Richter)
- Bad humour is an evasion of reality; good humour is an acceptance of it. (Malcolm Muggeridge)
- A joke is the shortest distance between two points of view. (Anon)
- Life does not cease to be funny when people die, any more than it ceases to be serious when people laugh. (Bernard Shaw)
- Humour, I have come to realise, is practically the only thing about which the English are utterly serious. (Malcolm Muggeridge)
- A total absence of humour makes life impossible. (Colette, French writer)
- A laugh a day keeps the heart attacks away. (Michael Miller, specialist in cardiology)
- A little nonsense now and then is relished by the best of men. (Anon)
- People without a sense of humour should never be put in charge of anything. (Robert Runcie)
- Humour and knowledge are the two great hopes of our culture. (Konrad Lorenz)
- I have always felt that the ability to laugh at oneself was an essential requirement for a sane existence in this world. (attributed to Prince Charles)
- The most wasted of all our days are those in which we have not laughed. (Anon)

- A pessimist forgets to laugh, but an optimist laughs to forget. (Anon)
- My brother (Bobus) and I have inverted the laws of nature. He rose by his gravity. I have sunk by my levity. (Canon Sydney Smith)
- Humour helps to keep things in perspective. (Ken Blanchard)
- Man is distinguished from all other creatures by the faculty of laughter. (Joshua Addison)
- No man was ever distinguished who could not bear to be laughed at. (Anon)

ILLUSTRATIONS
Keeping everyone's spirits up
No matter what turns up, he [Ernest Shackleton] is always ready to alter his plans and make fresh ones, and in the meantime laughs and jokes, and enjoys a joke with anyone, and in this way keeps everyone's spirits up.[2] (Frank Worsely)

Professional assessment
Laughter helps prevent some of the damage that stress causes to us. Not surprisingly it also makes us feel more relaxed ... Laughter is almost always a positive and beneficial thing ... We learn to laugh at four months of age, something that requires the action of fifteen facial muscles and changes in breathing. When we laugh, at first the heart rate rises, as does the rate of breathing. After laughter subsides there is a period of relaxation, easing muscle tension, which is useful in breaking the muscle spasm in some neuralgias and rheumatism. Laughter also aids lung ventilation, helping people with chest problems to clear mucus, although hearty laughter can make asthmatics wheeze. It can also, (very rarely indeed), if severe enough, induce a heart attack or a stroke. Extreme laughter gives body exercise. Laughter also improves alertness and memory. (Dr Patrick Dixon, *Signs of Revival*)

PRAYER
Lord, help us never to hurt people by our humour, and teach us how to use this gift of humour wisely and well. Grant us the right frame of mind to value all the good things you have given us, to enter into

all blessings you have promised to those who serve you, and to rejoice in the great mercy and grace you have showered upon us. For Christ's sake. Amen.

CHAPTER 15

People who recognise the significance of 'Presence'

Charisma for a leader has been defined as presence, passion, and a positive outlook on life.[1]

KNOWING THE SHEEP

John Wesley said 'the world is my parish' which was true for his unique calling, but there are not many Wesleys amongst us with quite such a wide sense of hands-on responsibility. Most of our congregations would prefer their leader to *know* their parish more and the world beyond a little less.

Good leaders know their followers, as the shepherd knows his sheep. The positive effect of the personal touch can never be exaggerated. Understanding this will seriously challenge the way leaders use their time, the placing of their desk in an office, and the car outside the office, their accessibility to visitors and phones, their frequency in being seen in the parish etc. To remember names too, is surely one of the greatest assets.

It is amazing the amount of 'feel' that one can gain from brushing shoulders with the people working within an organisation. So much is gleaned from the chit-chat about how things actually are; what casual visitors to the premises are concerned about, any current cynical jokes, their general mood, how new equipment is needed or how old equipment lacks attention; how tidy or untidy things are, or how people are facing up to their responsibility and fitting into the team. So much trouble can be avoided by tackling issues before they become problems and 'people' people have antennae for picking this up very quickly.

SEEING THE SHEPHERD

Without seeking to determine how today's leaders should appear in public it is worth drawing attention to the way a presenter was expected to appear for a certain TV advertising company in the USA:

> The company expects from its male guest advertisers clarity, warmth, total belief in the product, a neat appearance, no unsightly nasal hair (you will be in close up) no earrings or nose studs and truly clean fingernails with cuticles that are even and unchewed. We are committed to improving our customers' experience. You must be too.

Our appearance and manner in some circles can be off-putting and we should keep this in mind. This does not conflict with Samuel's comment to Jesse's family when choosing to anoint David for future leadership. He said, 'Don't judge by appearance or height …The LORD doesn't make decisions the way you do!' (1 Samuel 16:7 NLT). David had been hurried in from caring for the sheep in the fields, and was not dressed for public appearances, but something shone through. John the Baptist was dressed like a 1960s' hippie and people were drawn to him in the desert because there seemed to be revolutionary and long awaited tidings of a new kingdom being set up.

To a degree we dress appropriately out of respect for the company we keep or expect to meet. It is sensible in church not to be over-dressy as if wanting to show off the latest fashion. There was some good sense in the past practice for Church of England clergy of wearing a clean surplice over all and a black scarf, as laid down in the *Book of Common Prayer*. We are not commending a return to such particular attire nor necessarily an abandonment of the practice – so much depends upon the local situation. But the principle behind having a simple uniform dress always available for directing worship. In this way one leader would not be tempted to outdo another in style. Worshippers were not to be distracted by their leaders' latest fashion or lack of it, by the quality of cloth she was wearing, its state of repair or cleanliness.

But the way leaders dress before their people is much less important than the sense of their presence among their people.

QUOTES

- I have to be seen to be believed. (HRH Queen Elizabeth II)
- The ability to stop is an important trait of leaders' (Max DePree)
- The most important thing a captain can do is to see his ship through the eyes of his crew. (Anon)
- Leaders must communicate. Understanding without communication is futile. (Max DePree)
- Good coaching means being present, on the spot, constantly giving appropriate feedback on your players' performances. (Don Shula, *The Little Book of Coaching*)
- I always thought it was essential to look as if one was in control even if one wasn't. The most important thing is a degree of grip – even at the cost of being known as Hitler Hastings. I felt it was right that the editor should be feared as well as respected. (Max Hastings, one-time editor of the *Daily Telegraph*)
- His cardinal mistake is that he isolates himself, and allows nobody to see him; and by which he does not know what is going on in the very matter he is dealing with.[2] (Abraham Lincoln)
- A successful leader needs to have not only good speaking skills but good listening skills. Never pass up the opportunity to remain silent.[3] (Lt Gen Wimmial G. Pagonis)
- The most important thing a captain can do is to see his ship through the eyes of his crew. (Anon)
- While pastors of growing churches are usually not 'people persons' who lose themselves in interaction with individuals, yet on average they are somewhat more relationship-partnership-orientated than their colleagues in declining churches. (Christian A. Schwarz)
- A certain amount of heart is required of a captain; aloofness at any rate is not a quality that goes down well with the average cricket team. (Mike Brearley)

ILLUSTRATIONS
Leading by wandering around
It is a vital principle for leaders to keep close to the people. This has

been dubbed MBWA – *Managing By Wandering Around.* They call it 'roving leadership', 'being in touch' and 'getting out of the ivory tower'. It simply involves stepping out, interacting with people, and establishing human contact. Politicians refer to it as 'touching the flesh'. Peters and Waterman called it 'the technology of the obvious'.[4]

In the field of action

President Abraham Lincoln had a practice of being out on the field, meeting with people from whom he could receive impressions, reports, complaints and ideas first hand. In the process he complimented them, commented on what they were doing, praised their contribution, encouraged, joked and thanked individuals personally for their help, involvement, sacrifice. He also verbally spread the message of what he aimed to achieve for them and their country. He made face to face communication with as many people as possible, his leaders, workers, the grieving parents of soldiers lost in the war, soldiers in training and soldiers on the battle field, and patients and staff in hospitals etc. This was the cornerstone of his personal leadership thinking – an approach that would become part of a revolution in leadership philosophy 100 years later.[5] (D. T. Phillips)

Knowing one's followers

Napoleon Bonaparte, one of the world's greatest and best known leaders, knew every officer in his army by name. He liked to wander through the camp, meet an officer, greet him by name, and discuss some battle or manoeuvre in which he knew that that particular soldier had been engaged. He never missed an opportunity to enquire about a soldier's home town, wife or family. His men never ceased to be amazed by the detailed personal information he remembered about them. Since his men appreciated his great interest in them it was easy to understand the devotion they felt for him in return.

Front-line leader

Field Marshal Montgomery was able to turn the tide of falling morale in the Eighth Army North Africa campaign during the Second World War by setting his headquarters in a caravan up-front where he could be seen by his troops. With this technique he prepared them to gain the upper hand over the enemy commanded by Field Marshal Rommel.

Sir Ernest Shackleton made himself accessible to his crew, listened to his men's concerns, and kept them informed about his ship's business.[6] (Orde-Lees)

The secret of the Viet Cong's ultimate victory

Concerning Ho Chi Minh's military leaders and their twenty-five year survival and ultimate victory John Roy said, 'There is nothing to distinguish their generals from their private soldiers except for the star they wear on their collars ... their colonels go on foot like privates. They live on the rice they carry on them, or the tubers they pull out of the forest earth, on the fish they catch ... No pre-packaged rations, no cars or fluttering pennants ... no military bands. But victory![7]

Benefit of 'Presence'

Observe people wherever you happen to meet them, not just in church situations. You can learn a great deal about a person at a restaurant, on a sports' field, in his home or his garden.

Many years ago, when the late President Eisenhower was vacationing in Denver, his attention was called to an open letter in a local newspaper, which told how a six-year-old boy, Paul Haley, dying of incurable cancer, had expressed a wish to see the President of the United States. In one of those gracious gestures remembered long after a man's most carefully prepared speeches are forgotten, the President spontaneously decided to grant the boy's request.

On the Sunday morning, a big limousine pulled up outside the Haley home and out stepped the President. He walked up to the door and knocked. Mr Donald Haley opened the door, wearing blue jeans, an old shirt, and a day's growth of beard, totally unprepared for such a visitation. Behind him was his little son, Paul. The amazement at finding President Eisenhower on their doorstep can be imagined.

'Paul,' said the President to the little boy, 'I understand you wanted to see me. Glad to see you.' Then he shook hands with the six-year-old, took him out to see the presidential limousine, shook hands again, and left.

The Haleys and their neighbours, and a lot of other people did not forget that thoughtful deed by a busy President, for a long time to come. (Billy Graham)

Bush and the Texas Rangers

There is a story about George W. Bush and the Texas Rangers baseball team before he became the Governor of Texas and then the President of the United States. He was a baseball fan and rejoiced at the opportunity to organise the purchase of the Texas Rangers stadium of 80 million dollars. He then had the stadium rebuilt in 1994. No one loved it as he did. Rather than watch the games from an enclosed suite, which was the standard practice for most owners, Bush preferred to sit with the fans. He said he wanted to see them 'sitting in the seat they sat in, eating the same popcorn, peeing in the same urinal.' He would position himself behind the Rangers' dugout - section 109, Row 11 - and eat peanuts while he got to know the rowdiest fan, the hot-dog vendors, and even the ticket-takers by their first names. (Stephen Mansfield, *The Faith of George W. Bush*)

Limitations of 'Presence'

- There is something in the role of a pastor that says the pastor should always be available. (Ed Bratcher)
- If you're always available you're never available. (Ed Young)
- Today, the degradation of the inner life is symbolised by the fact that the only place sacred from interruption is the private toilet. (Lewis Mumford)

Too busy for people

Initially Dan held the position of intern. I remember one day soon after he started the job, I was standing in the office lobby having a conversation with a group of people, and Dan came in from the car park with his carefully arranged briefcase. He walked right through the group of us and didn't say a word. He strode down the hallway directly to his office. I excused myself from the group and followed him. Dan set his briefcase down on his desk, and when he turned around, he was surprised to see that I was standing there.

'Dan,' I said, 'what are you doing? You walked right by us, and you didn't say a word to anyone.'

'Well, I have a lot of work to do,' Dan answered, pulling out a stack of papers.

'Dan,' I said, looking him in the eyes, 'you just passed your work.'

I wanted him to understand that people must come first to a leader. (John C. Maxwell)

Avoiding the people
I'll gladly climb the terrible stair
That leads up to the terrible steeple
But I won't go down the terrible street
That leads to the terrible people.
(Anon)

Laughter from a Cloud
I wish I loved the Human Race;
I wish I loved its silly face;
I wish I liked the way it walks;
I wish I liked the way it talks;
And when I'm introduced to one
I wish I thought *What Jolly Fun*!
(Sir Walter A. Raleigh (1861–1922)
in his *Wishes of an Elderly Man*)

God among his people
I sought to hear the voice of God
I climbed the highest steeple
And God declared 'Go down again'
I dwell among the people. (Anon)

PRAYER
Lord, there were holy days and nights you spent in prayer and hectic days you spent with people. Help me to recognise the relevance and right times for both. For Christ's sake. Amen.

CHAPTER 16

People who thank and encourage others

'The tongue of the wise is health.'
(PROVERBS 12:18b KJV)

'Heaviness in the heart of a man maketh it stoop:
but a good word maketh it glad.'
(PROVERBS 12:25 KJV)

'A word fitly spoken is like apples of gold in pictures of silver.'
(PROVERBS 25:11 KJV)

NEED FOR GIVING ENCOURAGEMENT

The old style in the Navy was never to commend anything that was well done; to do well was considered to be no more than a man's duty. On the other hand anything that was badly done led to a severe reprimand. (*The Making of an Admiral* contained in *The Memoirs of Lord Charles Beresford*, 1914)

Beresford was a very popular British admiral who served at the beginning of 20th century. He pioneered a reversal of the traditional practice saying that 'Any smart action performed by an officer or man should be appreciated publicly by signal. This is complimentary to the officer or man and to the ship in which he is serving at the time. Everyone is grateful for appreciation.'

Everyone needs encouragement. It pleasurably affirms our self-worth and converts our lethargy into new sources of energy. Tragically this simple gesture can be ignored in the belief that people serving the Lord don't need appreciating – after all aren't they are doing their work for him?

But leaders give encouragement on the Lord's behalf also. In thanking others and encouraging them by deliberately underlining how much they are appreciated, they will find it produces an almost magical effect. It not only creates a bond of mutual respect, it stimulates a 'feel-good factor' between the leaders and those being led. It also 'empowers' people, and makes the service of God a joy. It gives a clear message too that the leaders are not trying to take any credit for success to themselves.

NEED FOR RECEIVING ENCOURAGEMENT

Some leaders find it hard to give praise because they are often very uneasy about receiving it. This can have a double negative effect. When we cannot accept other people's genuine compliments they feel downcast because their positive gesture seems to have been thrown back at them. Leaders not only must learn to give praise but also to learn how to receive it, and register it in one's emotional bank. It is useful to note how one feels about it a week later.

QUOTES

- 'Do not withhold good from those who deserve it, when it is in your power to act.' (Proverbs 3:27 NIV)
- 'Give to everyone what you owe: if you owe taxes, pay taxes; if respect, then respect; if honour, then honour.' (Romans 13:7 TNIV)
- Encouragement is the oxygen of the soul. (John C. Maxwell)
- People will want to know that I care, before they care about what I know. (Anon)
- Giving recognition costs nothing. Yet it is one of the most overlooked and least used tools of motivation a leader has at his disposal.[1] (Myron Rush)
- If you need more Sunday School teachers, make heroes out of the ones you already have. (Anon. vicar)
- Next to excellence is the appreciation of it. (William Makepiece Thackery)
- When you don't know what to say – say thank you. (Anon)
- To thank someone is to show our dependence upon them. (Anon)
- It is wiser to administer a fleet by commendation than by condemnation. (Admiral Lord Charles Beresford)
- 'You done splendid!' (Casey Stengel's accolade reserved for

his best players)

- Some mentors and leaders offer praise too freely, or too unctuously, so that it becomes devalued. (Mike Brearley)

ILLUSTRATIONS
Extraordinarily personable

He is good at remembering what you said and what matters to you. A good point made to him in a meeting results in a hand written note from him being delivered by the US Embassy the following week, saying how much he appreciated it and has been thinking about it. (William Hague writing about the leadership qualities of President George W. Bush, *Sunday Telegraph*, 6 October 2002)

Better work and greater work

I have yet to find a man, however exalted in his station, who did not do better work and put forth greater effort under a spirit of approval than under a spirit of criticism. (Charles M. Schwab)

Encouraging the man who failed

A very worried businessman came to see Myron Rush because he was afraid he was going to be fired from his job. Myron was surprised because he knew his friend's boss and had heard him speak highly of this businessman often.

'Why's that?' Myron asked.

'I have failed to keep my inventory under control. As a result, at the end of the year, my division ended up being several thousand dollars in the red,' he replied.

When the president of the company called and wanted to see him the next morning, he assumed he was to be sacked. Myron offered some encouraging words and promised he would do all he could to help if he ever needed a new position.

Later the man called him back to thank him and tell him, 'I won't be needing another job. The president just wanted to assure me personally that he still had confidence in my ability to manage the division. He thought I might be needing some encouragement after the bad year I had just had. One thing I'm certain about. I won't be letting my boss down. If he thinks I can do a good job I'll prove he's right.'

Apparently the next year this man's division earned the largest profit in the entire corporation. (Myron Rush, *Management: A Biblical Approach*)

Revenge thing

One Sunday morning in church the preacher ended his sermon by reading the first chapter of *Jesus for a New Generation* by Kevin Ford. The congregation was riveted. It told the story of a young man called Rex, through the lips of his sister, Jodie.

Rex had returned to live at home because he had failed to make a go of it on his own. He was withdrawn and seemed always to be arguing with his parents. His mother treated him like a child even though he was twenty. She would tell him to clean his room, tuck his shirt in and comb his hair. His father, an aggressive, successful businessman, would tell him to go out and make something of his life. He used to refer to his son as The Slob because he didn't share his values. He'd tell Rex's sister Jodie, to call The Slob to dinner, or he'd say to Rex, 'Hey, you! The Slob! Move your big head! I can't see the TV.'

The shock awaiting them

One Christmas Rex's mother and sister went shopping and had a big row about Rex. His sister felt that he shouldn't be treated so badly by his parents when he was obviously depressed.

Arriving home from the shops Rex's mother suddenly began to scream. Jodie had never heard anyone scream like that in her whole life – not even in a horror movie. She dialled 999 and the police arrived. Rex had taken his father's shotgun, put the barrel under his chin and blown his head off. Jodie said that she thought that Rex had done it to get even with his parents.

It was a revenge thing – an anger thing more than a depression thing. He left a note and well, it was a real twist of the knife. In it he said, 'Mum, sorry I left the room in such a mess. Left my shirt untucked, too. And Dad, remember how you were always telling me to move my big head? Well, I blew my big head away, Ha-ha! Have a nice life!

Your son,

The Slob.

Putting it down on paper

Helen Morsia, a teaching nun, tells of the day her kids were fighting in class. So she made them all sit down, take out a piece of paper, list the names of all their fellow students and write something positive they liked about each of them. Then she collected them up and writing the name of each student at the top of separate pieces of paper, listed all the nice things the other students had said about them and gave the appropriate comments to each of them. The students read them in amazement, making remarks like: 'I never knew they felt that way!'

Helen moved away, but years later, when she came home on vacation, her father said to her, 'The Ecklands called last night to say their son, Mark, was killed in Vietnam and they'd like you to come to the funeral.'

After the service, Mark's former classmates, and Helen, gathered in the family home. Suddenly Mark's father said to her, 'I'd like to show you something. I found this in my son's wallet.' Opening the wallet he removed a piece of paper, now yellow and worn, listing, in Helen's handwriting, all the good things his classmates had said about him fifteen years before. Then one by one, smiling sheepishly, all the others opened their purses and wallets and produced theirs too. Helen was simply reduced to tears.

To think that a boy would carry around such an old piece of paper everywhere he went – even to his death in a paddy field on the other side of the world!

Of course the paper was very significant for him, it had some all-too-rare words of appreciation which had encouraged him so much, as indeed all his class-mates had been by theirs.

What's in a name?

During my second month of nursing school, our professor gave us a 'pop quiz'. I was a conscientious student and had breezed through the questions, until I read the last one: 'What is the first name of the woman who cleans the school?' Surely this was some kind of a joke!

I had seen the cleaning woman several times. She was tall, dark-haired and in her 50s, but how would I know her name? I handed in my paper, leaving the last question a blank.

Before class ended, one student asked if the last question would count toward our class grade. 'Absolutely,' said the professor, who continued: 'In your careers you will meet many people. *All* are significant. They deserve your attention and care, even if all you do is smile and say "Hello!"' I've never forgotten that lesson. I also learned that the cleaner's name was Dorothy. (Anon)

In the school play

A little boy was desperate to have a part in his school play. His mother feared he could never be chosen and would be very disappointed not to be given a part. When his teacher saw his zeal she asked him if he was any good at clapping? He assured her he was. She asked him to show her how he did it. The little boy clapped his little hands together as loudly as he could. The teacher appeared surprised and murmured approvingly.

On the day the parts were awarded the little boy rushed up to his mother after school, his eyes shining with pride and excitement. 'Guess what, Mum,' he shouted. 'I've got a part in the play. I've been chosen to clap and cheer.' (Anon)

Everyone loves encouragement

A fisherman looked over the side of his boat and saw a snake with a frog in its mouth. Feeling sorry for the frog, he reached down and gently removed it from the snake's mouth and let it go free in the water.

But then he felt sorry for the hungry snake. Having no food on board, he took a flask of bourbon and poured a few drops into the snake's mouth. The snake swam away looking happy, the frog was clearly happy to be free, and the fisherman was happy for having performed such good deeds.

Thinking all was now well he settled down to fish when, after a few minutes, he heard a knocking against the side of the boat. The fisherman looked down and was amazed to see the snake was back again – this time with two frogs in its mouth.

Praise the simple things

The Americans needed a pen that they could use to write in space. Over ten years they spent 18 million dollars inventing one. The Russians used a pencil.

GIVE CREDIT WHERE CREDIT IS DUE
If you know that praise is due him
Now is the time to give it to him.
For hwe cannot read his tombstone when he is dead

THOUGHT FOR THE DAY
Those who bring sunshine to the lives of others cannot keep it from
themselves.

PRAYER
Lord, your Holy Spirit is our Encourager. Help us also to encourage
others on your behalf. Amen.

CHAPTER 17

People who negotiate change constructively

We are living in an era of accelerated change.
(ALVIN TOFLER, FUTURE SHOCK)

Leadership is inextricably connected with the process of innovation, bringing new ideas, methods, or solutions into use.
(KOUZES & POSNER)

If you believe that something must change then you must change it, no matter if there are risks.
(JOSE LUIS GUERRERO, TRADE UNION LEADER IN MEXICO)

I'm looking for a lot of men with an infinite capacity for not knowing what can't be done.
(HENRY FORD)

SEEN MANY CHANGES

A new bishop was greeted at the door of a local church by an elderly man who claimed that he had been the verger there for over fifty years.

'Oh,' responded the bishop, 'you must have seen a good many changes during all that time.'

'Oh yeah, Bishop, that I hev' – an' Oi've resisted every one of 'em!'

Change is one of the most sensitive areas for any leader to negotiate. People change, language changes, times change, fashions change, tastes change, and cultures change; organisations and churches must change to keep up.

But tradition being such a rich inheritance in the church, some of it can be discarded at too great a cost. Yet to use our rich traditions as a selling point in this day and age may be to create the impression to outsiders that the church is quaintly irrelevant for them and their children.

CHANGE IS ESSENTIAL FOR SURVIVAL AND SUCCESS

Change is necessary for winning battles. Admiral Nelson was insistent that everything on board not necessary for winning the battle should be taken off the ship. In how many ways are our churches cluttered with paraphernalia, which hinders us from tackling the challenges around us? And how many churches are impeded by top-heavy leadership and out-of-date infrastructures?

Change is essential for survival, but we must never make a change for change's sake, nor exaggerate the effects of the changes we expect to make.

If a new leader goes to an organisation or congregation with just a tiny remnant of elderly members trying to keep things going, then maybe any change with the slightest hope of doing some good will be welcomed, but much prayer and great sensitivity is needed. It's not always wise to follow the advice given to a young American pastor, 'Make all the changes you can in the first six months whilst you are still in the honeymoon phase.' The church you have just arrived to lead may be still in the grieving stage over the loss of their last pastor and any change is seen as a smirch on his memory.

New leaders taking over an organisation or a congregation which is running at full speed, like a passenger liner in mid-ocean, are heading for trouble if a turnaround cannot clearly be justified, and reasonable notice for preparation has not been widely published.

Just the fact of having a new leader introduces spontaneous changes, of which the leader may him/herself be totally unaware. Things are carrying on as normal as far as they are concerned. They may be unaware of the particular style or foibles of the previous leader. Any changes caused just through a fresh approach is quite a challenge for some of the faithful to cope with, and may create repercussions that can take years to heal.

HIS PLACE IS FILLED BUT HIS SPACE IS EMPTY

The departure of the previous leader will have already disturbed the chemistry of the rest of the leadership group who may well be feeling insecure. And when the new leader wants to effect alterations quickly, the level of dependability and loyalty may seem lower than expected. Attempts at rapid change can provoke a good deal of unpleasant and unexpected resistance.

Again, leaders need to beware of giving the impression that they are using the organisation or congregation as a platform for promoting their own special line, and leave the people feeling that they are to be unwilling guinea pigs for an unwanted experiment!

A new leader has come to the organisation with a good stock of credibility in the bank, but this can be quickly dissipated by unwise, unnecessary, untimely and unpopular changes.

THE MAKE-UP OF THE ORGANISATION

However, assuming that change is clearly seen to be necessary and desirable to the main leadership bodies in the organisation, it is helpful for the leadership to realise that every church or organisation is composed of four main groupings, radicals, progressives, conservatives and traditionalists. To understand this will help any leader to be prepared for change as constructively as possible.

Radicals tend to react initially at an emotional level. They are always ready to get up and have a go. They like the fast lane. They can resource good ideas but are sometimes very tempted to promote extremes that are of no interest to the main body. Their readiness to take risks will cause them to be regarded as reckless and irresponsible in the eyes of the rest of the organisation.

Progressives tend to react rationally. They accept the need for moderate change and are quick to grasp the benefits of a good idea. They are willing to take risks and promote changes provided there is a reasonable case and responsible planning. This is a vital group to identify in an organisation or congregation.

Conservatives also tend to react at a rational level. Their natural disposition is *laissez faire* – let sleeping dogs lie. They tend to support the *status quo* and to maintain it responsibly. They like everything to be well under control and are not, by nature, risk-takers. The leadership needs these people on their side. Once convinced they are willing to co-operate and to contribute a fair share to the financial burden for the project.

Traditionalists, like the radicals, tend to react emotionally. Their identity and their security are in their traditions. They are usually very threatened by the merest hint of change and they resist it in every possible way. They are hard to win over, but may eventually be won over by love and care.

Leaders often think these are the ones to concentrate on convincing, when it would be wiser to invest most of one's time listening to and convincing the conservatives. They are winnable. Get them on one's side, and, if it comes to votes, the new vision will eventually carry the day. But always bend over backwards, without being two-faced, to find ways of showing the traditionalists that they are loved, listened to and provided for, as far as is humanly possible. It is always unwise to change things too soon, too often – and to make too many changes all at once.

QUOTES

- Change was never necessary and always evil. (Robert 'Jimmy' James, famous Headmaster of Harrow School)
- Social change never stops ... We are not free to choose to avoid dealing with change. (Max DePree)
- When you have a real innovation don't compromise. (Peter Drucker)
- Probably the most important preparation for change is lavish communication. (Max Depree)
- It's hard to change things where nothing is moving at all. (Anon)
- Leaders always find a way to make things happen. (John Maxwell)
- The less effective executives were those who plunged into major commitments before they had built adequate support. (John P. Cotter and Paul R. Lawrence, *Mayors in Action*, John Wiley and Sons, 1974)
- Not since he once wished viewers a Happy New Year has Frank Bough ever quite said precisely what he means. (Dennis Potter)
- Everyone talks of changing the world, but no one talks of changing himself. (Leo Tolstoy)
- The truth is that implementing change will only happen freely and fruitfully where personal growth and change are taking place in the leader. (Robert Warren)
- To live is to change, and a changing church is a sign of life within. (George Carey)

ILLUSTRATIONS
Unprepared for the change

I arrived at work one morning with a long list of telephone calls to make. As I turned to my telephone, I discovered that my old phone with its thirty-six familiar buttons had been replaced by a gadget with an LCD display that looked like nothing I had ever touched before. I asked my executive assistant what this gadget was and found out that it was, in fact, my new telephone.

'But I didn't ask for a new telephone,' I said.

'Well,' Carol responded, 'everybody's got one.'

At 3 p.m. I was to be trained in its operation. I asked Carol if she could speed things up. I had a lot of work to do.

Within minutes, Sally arrived and told me cheerfully that she was here to teach me how to use the new phone. Her first question was, 'Are you computer literate?'

I wasn't.

'Can you read the instructions on the screen?'

Well, I couldn't.

She turned up the brightness. I still couldn't read the thing.

'In that case,' she said ... (Remember, this man had one of the most senior positions in the company), 'perhaps you can't have a telephone.'

When I asked for my old phone back, Sally told me that it had already been junked. At this point, I was becoming a little perturbed. I really didn't want to change to a phone that rang with the tune 'Mary had a little lamb'. Carol, sensing that warfare was about to erupt, stepped in and said she would work on the problem. Sally left.

A few hours later a young man walked into my office, where I was holding a meeting. As if we weren't there, he lay down on the floor and began to work on the cabling of the new telephone. I inquired, as civilly as I could, what he was doing. He told me in a matter of fact way, 'Sally said you didn't want a telephone that rings "Mary had a little lamb" and I'm changing it to the "Battle Hymn of the Republic".'

Believe me, when no one is paving the way, change is tough to take. (Max DePree)

The King James Version of the Bible

When the King James Version of the Bible was issued in 1611 many of the clergy objected. Archbishop Richard Bancroft (Canterbury) said, 'Tell his majesty that I had rather be rent to pieces with wild horses than any such translation by my consent should be urged upon poor churches.' (Gustavus S. Paine, *The Men Behind the KJV*)

Reaction to open-air evangelism

Following some evangelistic preaching at Moorfields, near London, George Whitefield (1714–70) attended a service at the local parish church and found himself the subject of the sermon.

The preacher, the Rev Dr Joseph Trapp, one of London's ablest clergy, denounced Whitefield's preaching, ridiculing his writing and accusing him of dishonesty. Later, his biographer wrote, 'This attack confirmed Whitefield in his belief that he could expect nothing but opposition from the clergy and that God was thus thrusting him out into the fields.' (Arnold Dallimore)

Radio evangelism

According to Clarence Jones, co-founder of the Christian Broadcasting station HCJB, in Ecuador, the idea of promoting the gospel by means of radio was greeted with a chorus of objections from other Christian groups with such comments as, 'Will God prosper this new-fangled fad since it operates in the very realm of Satan – the air? Don't the Scriptures clearly portray the devil as the prince of the power of the air?'

New trends in church music

An American church leader wrote complaining of the modern trends in church music:

'There are several reasons for opposing it', he writes. 'One, it's too new. Two, it's often worldly, even blasphemous. The new Christian music is not as pleasant as the more established style. Because there are so many new songs, you can't learn them all. It puts too much emphasis on instrumental music rather than godly lyrics. This new music creates disturbances making people act indecently and disorderly. The preceding generation got along without it. It's a money-making scene and some of these new music upstarts are lewd and loose.[1] (An American pastor in 1723 attacking Isaac Watts, the father of American hymnody!)

Sunday Schools for children

The Sunday School movement was started by Robert Raikes (1735–1811) who was moved to do something to improve the neglected condition of the local children in Gloucester, and their behaviour on Sundays. He helped in the establishment of a Sunday School in his own parish (open on week-days and Sundays) for the teaching of scripture, reading and other elementary subjects. He faced a lot of opposition from traditionalist Christians who felt that popular education spelled revolution. He was also opposed by the clergy under the leadership of the Archbishop of Canterbury, who summoned his bishops to see what could be done to stop him, for he believed Raikes was violating the Sabbath (Exodus 20:8).

Likewise, as the movement spread to North America, a pastor said of a class held in his church on Sunday, 'You imps of Satan, doing the devil's work. I'll have you set in the street.[2] (C. B. Every)

Organ music

I happen to enjoy organ music but it has to be admitted that it does not appeal to our post-modern generation. For churches to keep young people today, and attract new ones sensitive changes have to be made. Visiting Canada recently I was discussing this problem with an Anglican bishop and he told me of a local town where, every weekend, the residents round the main square were disturbed by a rowdy gathering of young people.

A meeting of the town's elders was arranged and police advice sought. It seemed that very little could be done about it, especially when the police were hesitant about having a set-to with the noisy crowd. Finally, an old man on the council begged to be given the chance to resolve the problem and asked for a three months' trial. The others readily agreed, wondering how on earth he expected to tackle such a tricky problem!

The old man fixed up a PA system all round the square and every Friday, Saturday and Sunday evening he relayed organ music across the square. The young people had completely abandoned the place by the end of three weeks and the local residents relaxed once more in peace.

P.S. Actually there was quite a rumpus in many of our 18th century churches when organs began to replace the local fiddlers and singers who had traditionally led the music from the west-end gallery, whither the congregation 'turned to face the music' at the appropriate time for congregational singing. Even one Archbishop of York publicly communicated his disgust at the changes taking place.

Overtaken by change

In the 1940s, 80 per cent of all watches sold were made in Switzerland. In the late 1950s, the digital watch was presented to them, but they rejected it because they already had the best watches and the best watchmakers in the world. Then the man who developed the digital watch, now a worldwide success, sold his idea to Seiko.

In 1940, Swiss watch companies employed 80,000 people. Today they employ 18,000. In 1940 they made 80 per cent of all watches sold. Today they make 20 per cent – and the majority are digital!

The secret of change

The key is to realise that within any organisation there are different types and groups of people. They (all) see change, and respond to it differently. If we can understand what those differences are, then we can facilitate, rather than frustrate, the changes we are seeking to implement. (Robert Warren)

PRAYER

Lord grant me the serenity to accept the things I cannot change, the courage to change the things I can, and the wisdom to know the difference. (Reinhold Niebuhr, adapted)

CHAPTER 18

People who face up to confrontation

AREAS NEEDING A LEADER'S INTERVENTION
The areas which need a leader's intervention usually fall into four main categories, belief, behaviour, misunderstanding, and mismanagement.

Belief and behaviour
Concerning the first two, these are best resolved by following the procedures spelt out by Jesus himself:

> 'Moreover if your brother sins against you, go and tell him his fault between you and him alone. If he hears you, you have gained your brother. But if he will not hear, take with you one or two more, that "by the mouth of two or three witnesses every word may be established". And if he refuses to hear them, tell it to the church. But if he refuses even to hear the church, let him be to you like a heathen and a tax collector.
>
> 'Assuredly, I say to you, whatever you bind on earth will be bound in heaven, and whatever you loose on earth will be loosed in heaven. Again I say to you that if two of you agree on earth concerning anything that they ask, it will be done for them by My Father in heaven. For where two or three are gathered together in My name, I am there in the midst of them.'
>
> Then Peter came to Him and said, 'Lord, how often shall my brother sin against me, and I forgive him? Up to seven times?'
>
> Jesus said to him, 'I do not say to you, up to seven times, but up to seventy times seven.' (Matthew 18:15–22 NKJV)

Misunderstanding

This is a frequent problem area, usually caused by lack of proper communication.

The best way to handle such a situation is to bring the parties together in as relaxed a way as possible. Then ask each what was actually said and what was actually meant. Whether the perceived misunderstanding was intended or not, where any apologies are called for, they should, of course, be exchanged. The parties should then shake hands as a token that all is now clear, settled and over.

Mismanagement

Of all the aspects of leadership, probably the most disagreeable is having to grasp nettles, but that is exactly what followers look to their leaders to do. This may even involve personal confrontation with some very significant people in the organisation or church.

Difficult? Yes, difficult indeed! The only people I know who handle confrontation matter-of-factly are those drill sergeants whose objective seems to be to bully the troops under them into a terrified jelly of dehumanising compliance! Hardly suitable in a church! Confrontation is never easy but it has to be handled sooner rather than later - and usually the sooner the better. It is wiser to build a fence at the top of a cliff than a first aid post at the bottom!

The manner and motive of the drill sergeant is no model for a minister or a leader who wants to build up people in a positive way, and to teach them by example how to cope with confrontation in a Christ-like way.

TEN COMMANDMENTS FOR CLARIFICATION

In his book, *The Leadership Within You*, John Maxwell suggests using the term 'clarification' in place of 'confrontation' as a better approach all round. I find his Ten Commandments for Clarification very helpful and have adapted and abbreviated them as follows:

1. Clarify personally and privately – not in public.
2. Clarify as quickly as possible
3. Clarify by commencing with thoughtful compliments and thankful appreciation of helpful services and personal sacrifices hitherto. (Proverbs 16:24)
4. Clarify by dealing with one issue at a time.

5. Avoid harping back to that issue after the next point for clarification has been raised.

6. Clarify only the cases of behaviour or situations which the person being confronted could change.

7. Clarify without the use of sarcasm or exaggeration.

8. Avoid all such words as 'never' and 'always', as the person being confronted will quickly think of exceptions to this charge and become defensive.

9. Clarify, if possible, by presenting criticism as a positive suggestion. Or present a problem and ask the person to think of some constructive way it might be resolved.

10. Clarify without apologising, as apology may be a distraction from the seriousness of the problem being confronted. It could leave the person being confronted with the impression the leader is uncertain of the issue.

PLANNING YOUR INTERVIEW
Preparing your attitude
Firstly pray for wisdom and grace.

One needs to remember that people inherently want to do a good job. Your aim is to encourage them with that attitude.

Richard Brown of Dallas says, 'I always apply a mental test before I go into these situations. I ask myself, "If I were on the receiving end of this message, would I think it was a fair thing to have said to me?"'

Preparing your mind
Make a mental check list:

- Identify the main issues involved, and avoid side issues.
- Be sure you are dealing with facts, and not guesses or hearsay.
- Determine how you will end it, both if things turn out well or if matters cannot be resolved

Following the advice above make the initial meeting private between you and the person involved. If this is unsuccessful arrange for someone to accompany you the next time. And if this is still unfruitful then the person may need to be removed from the post, possibly through a face-saving sideways move, assuming the mismanagement was in no way criminal. Make sure you understand your position in law.

QUOTES

- If we could only read the secret history of our enemies, we would find in each man's life sorrow and suffering enough to disarm all hostility. (Henry Wordsworth Longfellow)
- Seek first to understand, then to be understood. (Stephen Covey)
- Whereto serves mercy but to confront the visage of offence? (Shakespeare, *Hamlet*)
- Diplomacy is to do and say the nastiest thing in the nicest way. (Isaac Goldberg)
- When your partner is saying something, listen. Don't just think of what you are going to say next. (Juliet Janvrin)
- Use 'I feel' statements rather than 'you are' statements. (Juliet Janvrin)
- Bad leadership happens when leaders put their personal desires ahead of their good judgement. (Anon)
- When you have to clarify or confront be bold to speak the truth, but be sure to speak it in love (Ephesians 4:15). (Anon)
- An alarming parody of St John 8:32, 'You will know the truth and the truth will make you flee!' (Anon)
- Anger is like a stranger – it does not stay in one house. (African Proverb)
- People in a temper often say a lot of silly things they really mean. (Penelope Gilliatt)
- Anger is the wind that blows out the lamp of the mind. (Robert Ingersoll)
- No situation is so bad that losing your temper won't make it worse. (Anon)

ILLUSTRATIONS

The prophet Nathan confronts a king

The classic example of a well-handled confrontation is that of Nathan meeting King David after he had committed adultery with Bathsheba. David had also engineered the murder of her husband by placing him in the front of the battle.

Nathan gave David a report of two men in one city, one rich and the other poor. When a traveller called on the rich man he feasted him by taking the poor man's one little lamb. David was infuriated by such behaviour and vowed to see justice done. Then Nathan said to David, 'Thou art the man – thus saith the Lord God of Israel!' (see 2 Samuel 12:1–14)

Be emotionally prepared

One morning, en route to an early meeting with an employee who seemed to be bungling a project, the leader ran through a positive scenario in his mind. He asked questions and listened, to be sure he fully understood the situation, before trying to solve the problem. He anticipated feeling impatient, and rehearsed how he would handle such an emotion.

Gentle persuasion is better than force

A dispute once arose between the wind and the sun over which was the stronger of the two. There seemed no way of settling the issue. But suddenly they spotted a traveller coming down the road.

'This is our chance,' said the sun, 'to prove who is right. Whichever of us can remove the traveller's coat shall be deemed the stronger. And just to show you how sure I am, I'll let you have the first chance.'

So while the sun hid behind a cloud, the fierce wind then blew a strong icy blast. He blew and blew, but the harder he blew the more closely the traveller wrapped his coat around him. At last the wind gave up in disgust.

'Your turn,' said the wind.

The sun then came out from behind the cloud. He began to shine down upon the traveller with all his power. He shone brighter and brighter. The traveller felt the sun's genial warmth and as he grew warmer and warmer he began to loosen his coat. Finally, he was forced to take it off altogether and to sit down in the shade of the tree and fan himself.

'I win!' said the sun. (*Aesop's Fables*)

BIBLE EXHORTATIONS

'A soft answer turns away wrath,
But a harsh word stirs up anger.
The tongue of the wise uses knowledge rightly,
But the mouth of fools pours forth foolishness.'
(Proverbs 15:1,2 NKJV)

'Whatsoever things are true, whatsoever things are honest, whatsoever things are just, whatsoever things are pure, whatsoever things are lovely, whatsoever things are of good report ... think on these things.' (Philippians 4:8 KJV)

PRAYER

Lord, make me an instrument of your peace.
Where there is hatred, let me sow love,
Where there is injury, pardon,
Where there is discord, vision,
Where there is doubt, faith,
Where there is despair, hope,
Where there is darkness, light,
Where there is sadness, joy.
(Attributed to St. Francis of Assisi)

CHAPTER 19

People who cope with chaos, pain, failure and criticism

'For a just man falleth seven times, and riseth up again.'
(PROVERBS 24:16A KJV)

'He that hateth reproof shall die.'
(PROVERBS 15:10B KJV)

One reason why God created time was that there would be a place to bury the failures of the past.
(JAMES LONG)

Therefore since by the mercy of God we have this ministry, we do not loose heart.
(2 CORINTHIANS 4:1)

DON'T PANIC, PIKE!
King Attila the Hun warned his chieftains that they would often lose, regardless of how prepared they were to win. He continued, 'Lament, if necessary, but do not dwell too long on your bad moments lest they rise to rule your emotions forever.'

Upsets in life can be chaotic. Chaos is a nightmare, even for the temperamentally artistic with the untidy desk, but especially for the perfectionist who cannot relax till everything is under control once again.

NO EXCUSE FOR SHODDY WORK
Tom Peters wrote in 1979,

It may come as some consolation to frazzled executives that there have never been enough hours in the working day – the speed of business is the enemy of tidy rationality. Urgent phone calls interrupt long-planned meetings, noisy problems break into time allotted for quiet reflection, and before long, the orderly world of the executive's schedule is in shambles.

We are not putting forward excuses for shoddiness but acknowledging that in spite of being well prepared we will often meet situations for which we are completely unprepared, problems that were totally unpredictable.

Many leaders like to have ready-made solutions to hand before embarking on anything new. This may be practical in certain situations but there will always be the unpredictable ones. And some problems can never be solved quickly, if at all – as most parents know only too well. Home was not built in a day. Neither is church. In fact trying to resolve things too quickly is often counterproductive. Sometimes it is necessary to wait for the right solution, the right person, the right money and/or the right time.

PAIN

Leaders have to accustom themselves to coping with pain in all its forms, exhaustion, failure, misunderstanding, shame, and rejection by some, if not by all. Yet pain can be one of life's wake-up calls, an early warning of danger.

Someone with leprosy can lose nerve endings and ultimately break a limb or finger without knowing it. There are leprosy sufferers who pray constantly, 'Please God, let me feel the pain!' For them, pain is a gift from God; so it can be for us in certain areas of life.

The pain of failure can teach us lessons we would have no other way of learning. It may help to be reminded that 95 per cent of success is said to be built on failure. The first fifty years in the life of Churchill, Britain's most famous Englishman, have often been called 'A Study in Failure'! Besides his 'failures' Churchill frequently referred to his constant 'black dog' – dark periods of depression which added to his discomfort.

Pain may tempt us to give up altogether. But that is the one thing we must avoid if at all possible. Sir Ernest Shackleton has said, 'If you are a leader, a fellow that other fellows look to, you've just got to keep going.'

FAILURE

Failure plays an important role in success. 'Success does not breed success. It breeds failure. It is failure that breeds success.'[1] The greatest thing about failures is the good we can learn from them. Experience is what is left over after you have made the mistakes. Of course, we wouldn't have to learn all our lessons about failure from our own mistakes if we were willing to learn from the mistakes of others. An anonymous writer has given good advice, 'Learn from the mistakes of others. You will never live long enough to make them all yourself.' One advantage from reading the Bible, history, biographies or just listening, is that so much can be learned through the mistakes others have made and the lessons they learned from them.

However there is always the possibility of some of our own ventures failing. We cannot always predict with certainty how something will turn out. 'I have often marvelled at the thin line which separates success from any failure,' said Sir Ernest Shackleton.[2] But in any case there is still wisdom in the old maxim that if you never make a mistake you'll never make anything.

CRITICISM

This is part of the leadership package. Every leader has to undergo criticism which often feels like betrayal. No leader is unique for being criticised. Moses soon found himself being criticised, 'The whole congregation of the children of Israel murmured against Moses and Aaron in the wilderness.' (Numbers 16:2)

Even Jesus was frequently criticised, once notably by Judas Iscariot for letting Mary anoint him with costly ointment. Judas thought that this should have been sold for a large sum of money that could then have been given to the poor, even though Judas stole money from the commmmon bag for his own needs. 'Even my close friend, whom I trusted, has lifted up his heel against me.' (Psalm41)

So we are in very good company if we find ourselves unjustly criticised. But we do not deny that it can still be tough to take, especially when one feels one is giving one's all and the criticism is totallly undeserved and unjust.

Medicinal use of criticism

Thomas a Kempis once spoke of the medicinal use of criticism:

It's good that we at times endure opposition and that we are evilly and untruly judged when our actions and intentions are good, because often these experiences promote humility and protect us from vainglory. For then we seek God's witness to our heart.

Though criticism is painful, it may still be purposeful in God's plans. There are always people who seem to be destructively critical in the way they speak simply because they are unskilled in communicating: they have never observed it done constructively and well. They may be just feeling something deeply, but in trying to impress the listener with their depth of concern, they express it harshly. 'The British love to complain. The only trouble is they are not very good at it' (Simon Brooke). And judging by the tabloid newspapers destructive criticism sells well.

DISCERNMENT BETWEEN HOW IT IS SAID AND WHAT WAS SAID

Leaders need to discern what their critics are really trying to say so that they can address what is behind the complaint or criticism. However hurtfully it may have been expressed, there may be a good reason why it had to be said. Good leaders often have to handle change in some area of an organisation, and this tends to make people feel insecure, or worried, to which they respond angrily or aggressively.

Leaders have to bear criticism regarding actions taken for reasons that are often confidential. This means that, much as they would like to, they cannot make public why such steps were taken, resulting in faulty public perceptions of the reasons which have led to the particular course of action.

Then there are people who criticise simply because they are jealous of the leader's authority, and express this in personal attacks. 'Has the LORD spoken only by Moses? \Hath he not also spoken by us?' (Psalm 106:16 NIV).

The 'Tall Poppy' syndrome means there will always be criticism of those above us. The news media, rightly or wrongly, constantly criticises the United States of America, the tallest poppy in the field of nations today and the only super-power left in the world.

DISAGREEMENT WITH A LEADER

It is all right and perfectly natural for people to disagree with their leaders. We don't want churches full of zombies with no opinions of their own. However, members could make themselves better understood if they expressed their disagreements more agreeably.

One of our retired church members worked at a petrol service station and was asked by their head office if he would consider training new arrivals on how to answer complaints on the telephone, as it had been noticed how charmingly and disarmingly he always handled their clients' criticisms.

No leader can possibly please everyone, and it is worth noting that there will always be at least three per cent of people, at any given time, who are critical about something going on in any church, so leaders should never be surprised to find themselves criticised. It is par for the course!

RESPONDING TO CRITICISM

The late Tom Marshall lists a number of possible reasons as to why people become critical. Understanding these could help us handle the complaints constructively.

- **Fear of change or fear of the future.**
  If this is the problem it is simply a case for reassurance.
- **Mistakes, misunderstandings or lack of comprehension**
  Here there has obviously been a breakdown in communication and there is a need for further information.
- **Discouragement or despair**
  Such people need some personal attention to see where fresh encouragement and new hope might be remedial.
- **Internal disputes within the organisation or church**
  Tensions between personalities or departments, and differences about critical issues, need to be surfaced diplomatically and resolved positively.
- **Hurts and wounds inflicted by the leadership, either past or present**
  These may be the fault of the leader, or the perceptions of the led, but in either case they need to be resolved.
- **Wrong attitudes such as envy, jealousy or divisiveness**

Sooner or later these must be confronted constructively and decisively.

Watch your reaction

'If ever I get to Parliament' he [the boy William] muttered fiercely, 'I'll pass a lor against reports'³ (William Brown). We may empathise with his feelings, but feelings can blind us from seeing the appropriate responses.

There are numerous inappropriate reactions that fall into one or other of the following categories:

Defensiveness

Self-justification

Self-pity

Shifting blame on others in their absence

Understanding how we would react in similar circumstances will reveal how we might respond positively and responsibly.

QUOTES

- Creative people may be loyal to an idea but often appear to others to be non-joiners. (Anon)
- If we had to wait until everyone was agreed on everything before doing anything, there would be no such a thing as leadership. (Donald Rumsfeld, US Defence Secretary)
- We do not shrink from fair criticism. Criticism in the body politic is like pain in the human body. It is not pleasant but where would we be without it? (Winston Churchill)
- He always took criticism very, very mildly. One could say exactly what one liked in the way of criticism. He wanted the full critical value from his subordinates. (Comment from one of Winston Churchill's aides)
- This is a job where a thousand people are kicking your backside morning noon and night. (Prime Minister Tony Blair, 12 January 2004)
- To escape criticism, do nothing, say nothing, be nothing. (Elbert Hubbard)
- Fault-finding is dreadfully catching; one dog will set a whole kennel howling. (Charles Spurgeon)
- Never forget what a man says to you when he is angry. (Benjamin Disraeli)

- A thick skin is a gift from God. (Konrad Adenauer)
- It is impossible but that offences will come. (Jesus)
- Ninety-five per cent of success is built on failure. (Anon)
- A good leader learns to confront failure and learn from it. (Winston Churchill)
- God chooses what we go through. We choose how we go through it. (Victor Frankl, Holocaust survivor)
- Every night I court-marshal myself to see if I have done anything effective during the day. (Winston Churchill)
- I would rather fail in a cause that I know someday will triumph, than win in a cause I knew someday could fail. (President Woodrow Wilson)
- Those who fail to plan, plan to fail. (Proverb)
- Cheer up, the worst is yet to come. (Philaster Chase Johnson)
- The first rule for holes: When you are in one, stop digging. (Anon)
- How you rebound from a setback speaks volumes about who you are. (Ken Blanchard)
- Don't get a big head when you win, and don't let a broken heart get you down when you lose. (Anon)
- It takes a big person to admit a mistake and then go out of his or her way to right the wrong. (Ken Blanchard)
- For everything you miss you gain something else and for everything you gain you lose something. (Ralph Waldo Emerson)
- We forget that God is a specialist; he is well able to work our failures into his plans. (Pastor Erwin Lutzer)
- Success comes in cans; failure in can'ts. (Anon)
- Falling down does not make you a failure, but staying down does. (Anon)
- Success is never final; failure is never fatal; it is the courage to continue that counts. (Winston Churchill)
- I honestly think it is better to be a failure at something you love, than to be a success at something you hate. (George Burns)
- It is a mistake to suppose that men succeed through success; they much oftener succeed through failures. Precept, study, advice, and example could never have taught them so well

as failure has done. (Samuel Smiles)
- Never confuse a single mistake with a final mistake. (Anon)
- If only one could have two lives; the first in which to make one's mistakes, the second in which to profit by them. (D. H. Lawrence)
- Failure is one of my spiritual gifts. (John Maxwell)
- Leaders need to break through the information quarantine around them – the conspiracy to keep them pleased, even if uninformed. (Anon)
- I don't fear no one but God. Another boxer might knock me down but only God can make it permanent. (John Tate, US Boxer)
- Our problem is that we've tried to score too many goals. (Gordon Lee, Everton Manager)
- I resigned as a coach because of illness and fatigue. The fans were sick and tired of me. (John Ralston, Denver Broncos)
- You have to treat death like any other part of life. (Tom Sneva, Racing driver)
- I'm going to write a book, 'How to make a small fortune in Sport'. You have to start with a big one! (Ruby Carpenter, President of Philadelphia Phillies)
- Class in a football coach is, when they finally run you out of town, to look like you are leading the parade. (Bill Battle, sacked Tennessee manager)
- The referee counted too fast. (Chuck Olivares, explaining his knockout by Danny McAlinden)
- You've had over two thousand failures? No! I have had an education. (Thomas Edison, inventor of the light bulb)
- How else but through a broken heart may the Lord Christ enter in. (Oscar Wilde)
- Ah! There's no such thing as failure, Fred. You get around it. (Roland Tynon, Olympic athletic champion with two artificial legs, singer, medical doctor and hopeful senator, interviewed on the World Service of the BBC)
- If there's any single factor that makes for success in living, it is the ability to draw dividends from defeat. (William Marston)
- The things that hurt instruct. (Benjamin Franklin)
- While one person hesitates because he feels inferior, the

other is busy making mistakes and becoming superior.
- A failure is a man who blundered, but is not able to cash in on the experience. (Elbert Hubbard)
- We are all failures – at least, all the best of us are. (J. M. Barrie)
- The difference between greatness and mediocrity is often how an individual views a mistake. (Nelson Boswell)
- Many of life's failures are people who did not realise how close they were to success when they gave up. (Anon)
- Failure is not so bad if it doesn't attack the heart: success is all right if it doesn't go to the head. (Grantland Rice)
- Life is not simply holding a good hand: life is playing a poor hand well. (Danish Proverb)
- A man can fail many times but he isn't a failure until he begins to blame somebody. (John F. Kennedy)
- Meet success like a gentleman, and failure like a man. (Lord Birkenhead)
- The two hardest things to handle in life are failure and success. (Anon)
- Pain is a powerful teacher and a fantastic informer of our decision making process. (Bill Hybels)
- I am living proof that failure is good for you. (Michael Portillo, *Sunday Times*, 22 February 2004)

ILLUSTRATIONS
Jesus and his disciples
Some of Jesus' disciples failed to heal a young boy (Matthew 17:14–21) but Jesus continued to assign work to them and finally commissioned them to 'Go into all the world and preach the good news to all creation.' (Mark 16:15 NIV)

Peter disowned Jesus at his trial, despite his protests that he would never deny the Lord. When they met again in Galilee after the resurrection Jesus could have said that since he failed the last assignment he would have to be replaced, but instead he re-commissioned him. (John 21:15–22)

Learning from pain
Have you ever taken time to develop a 'Top Ten Pain List'? Sometimes in mentoring sessions with pastors, we sit around after

dinner and tell each other about the lessons we've learned the hard way. In sometimes humorous detail we describe stuff we'll never do again …

One guy said, 'I'll never make my mother-in-law the head elder again.'

Another pastor said, 'I'll never let a guest speaker teach on signs and wonders while I am on vacation.'

A particularly easy-going pastor said, 'I'll never again tell the worship dancer, "Just wear whatever you want when you dance at the morning service." Big mistake!'

These are all true pain-filled stories.[4] (Bill Hybels)

Learning from Failure

Rudolph Giuliani, ex-mayor of New York says:

> I am often my most severe critic. When I screw something up, I step out of myself (in a walk) and look at the errors I've made and agonise over why I didn't think of this or anticipate that. During the walk, I realised that I needed to resist that tendency, which was already building up. I said to myself, 'I can handle this. I am handling this. This is what I know how to do. This is what I was trained to do – to take charge, and make sound, sensible decisions.' This brief half hour of solitary meditation gave me a … feeling that I would get through it.

Learning from the cross

When the story of what has happened at St Thomas's Crookes is told it sounds immensely exciting. At the time it felt like that. However, for most of the time it has seemed very unlike that. Indeed out of it has come my conviction that if we are to know resurrection life and power and blessing in our service of God, there is only one point of learning for us: the only way that truth will become incarnated in us and in our leadership.

It will involve us in travelling to places of weakness, impotence, failure, risk, and the frontiers of the Kingdom of God. It is here, not in our 'successes' or achievements, but in our pain, in our discontent, and in our choosing to be vulnerable, that true learning takes place. Out of that comes the fruit and blessing which God alone gives. We express our faith by being willing to enter, indeed to pitch our tent and live, in the place of weakness.[5]

Undaunted by failure

Henry Ford, in 1914, started a very successful automobile manufacturing company and became famous for his production of the cheap popular Ford 8 people's car.

Charles Revson founded Revlon during the Great Depression by discovering a profitable market for high-fashion nail polish.

Samuel Moore Walton founded Wal-Mart to become the second richest citizen in the nation by 1984, through selling the greatest range of household goods at the cheapest price possible in his popular stores.

Yet, look at the records of these men.

Ford founded two companies that failed before he created the Ford Motor Company.

Charles Revson was living hand to mouth, moving from one dead-end job to another before he founded Revlon in 1932.

Walton lost his first store, a thriving business in Newport, Arkansas, to the landlord's son, because he failed to notice that his lease didn't include a renewal clause.

Wisdom from perseverance

The story is well known of Thomas Edison trying to develop an incandescent lamp, and his many, many failures in the process. Each new problem created more and more frustration for his laboratory assistants who began to have very negative attitudes towards the project. One of them finally suggested they give it up altogether.

'We have tried hundreds of experiments and none of them has worked. Let's face it, the thing's a failure!'

Edison replied, 'We have not failed once. We now know hundreds of things that won't work, so we are just that much closer to finding what will!'

Distorted views of failure

A vicar was interviewing a young man who was looking for a new position in charge of a daughter church. His final question was: 'Are you a responsible person?'

'Ah! Yes,' replied the applicant enthusiastically. 'I'm your man, vicar. In my last parish whenever anything went wrong they said I was responsible!'

The young man sadly didn't seem to have learned anything from his failures.. He hadn't taken them seriously enough.

Stanley Kubrick once made a film, *The Shining,* about a demented author (played by Jack Nicholson) typing the manuscript of his novel, haunted all the while, by the nightmare fear of failure. This man obviously took his failures far too seriously.

Brief biography of Abraham Lincoln
Difficult childhood
Less than one year formal schooling
Failed in business, 1831
Defeated for the legislature, 1832
Again failed in business, 1833
Elected to the legislature, 1834
Fiancée died, 1835
Defeated for Speaker, 1838
Defeated for Elector, 1840
Married, wife was a burden, 1842
Only one of his sons lived past the age of 18
Defeated for Congress, 1843
Elected to Congress, 1846
Defeated for Congress, 1848
Defeated for Senate, 1855
Defeated for Vice-President, 1856
Defeated for Senate, 1858
Elected President, 1860
(John Maxwell, *Your Attitude: Key to Success*)

Lincoln's solution
One of Abraham Lincoln's advisers said to him, 'Mr President, I cannot understand you. You treat your enemies with such kindness. I would have thought you needed to destroy them.'

Lincoln replied, 'I destroy my enemies when I make them into my friends.'

Biographical reflection

Looking back over his life and career during which he had lost many anguishing political battles, Senator G W Norris wrote years later,

> It happens very often that one tries to do something and fails. He feels discouraged, and yet he may discover years afterward that the very effort he made was the reason why somebody else took it up and succeeded. I really believe that whatever use I have been to progressive civilisation has been accomplished in the things I failed to do rather than in the things I actually did.[6]

Apology called for!

Don Shula, led the Miami Dolphins to five Super-Bowl appearances, and the Baltimore Colts to one more than any other coach in the National Football League.

He once lost his temper on national television in a heated game with the Los Angeles Rams. Unhappy with the referee's call, Shula voiced his displeasure in a string of blasphemous language that was heard in millions of American homes. As a result, he was flooded with letters from all over the country telling him how much he had let the supporters down.

Everyone who included a return address received an apology expressing his regret without excuse. 'Thank you for taking the time to write,' ran a typical response. 'Please accept my apologies for the remarks. I value your respect and will do my best to earn it again.'

Leaders live with rejection

One aspect of leadership not often mentioned is that of rejection. People, for whatever motives, will either accept or reject a leader. It is an occupational hazard. Leaders learn to live with it.

Brother Yun, called by God as a teenager to be a leader in the growing Chinese House Church Movement, was hounded from one community to another, imprisoned, beaten and tortured, but undeterred. 'We slept in caves and fled on foot from one place to another. Our hair was unkempt and our clothes were torn. People were disgusted with us and considered us "the scum of the earth and the refuse of the world."' (1 Corinthians 4:13)

Yet Brother Yun is still a leader whom thousands flock to hear.

Bigger than the game

People close to me will tell you I was not a real pleasant person after losing a football game, but I would have been a lot worse if I didn't realise something far bigger than football existed. I tried to attend Mass every morning. There's something good about kneeling down, asking help, and listening for answers ...

With a big picture perspective, adversity, circumstance, or even you own ego will not consume you. As a result you don't have to panic, give up, start to cheat, lose control, or begin to take uncalled-for risks to get the results you want right now.

Genuine faith is eminently practical, and that vast resource of inner knowing stands ready to assist today's leader who will exercise it. Faith in something bigger than you isn't passive emotion; it's an active belief that requires you to step onto the field and walk your talk.[7] (Don Shula)

Losing one's job

On losing his job as the editor of BBC Radio 4's *Today* Programme, Rob Little wrote:

> What I should be recalling are all my journalistic triumphs, the campaigning investigative reports and forensic interviews with lying or merely obfuscating politicians. But as is ever the case, it's the ghastly mistakes that stand out in my memory, the things that make one cringe ... That loneliness I mentioned has mostly gone now and instead I'm simply painfully aware that I've just given up the best job I'll ever have, and with a team of people I will miss more than I can adequately express.

The thin line between success and failure

I have given many lectures, and I do not deny that it gives me pleasure when the lecture goes well. One of my most vivid memories is of a lecture I gave many years ago, one of my worst failures.

It was at a university. I felt right from the first word that I was not going to make contact with my audience. I clung to my notes and laboriously recited with growing nervousness what I had to say. As the audience left I could see my friends slipping away hurriedly, to spare themselves the embarrassment of a meeting. On the way home with my wife I burst into tears.

But the next day a professor of philosophy called me on the telephone. He told me he had listened in his life to a large number of remarkable lectures. He had never heard one as bad as mine, he added, and this is what intrigued him and made him want to see me. This incident was the beginning of a wonderful friendship between us. I was the witness of his conversion to the Christian faith, and that was the source of more lasting joy to me than could ever have been procured by success in delivering a lecture. (Paul Tournier, *Adventures in Living*)

A wise way to handle criticism

Gideon was raised up by God to defeat the oppressive Midianites. Following the Lord's instructions he was able to do this with just a handful of men. To his great surprise, instead of kind words of gratitude he received harsh words of criticism. The Ephraimites, who were on his side, were affronted because he had not invited them to join his victorious team.

Why had he overlooked them? What had they done wrong? Did he think they were weaklings? They criticised him sharply. It is worth reading the clever way in which he was able to mollify them and put things right. (Judges 8:11)

Merely a misunderstanding

Once upon a time a man had a log cabin in the mountains, which he reached by Landrover. Every weekend he would drive up to his cabin along a very dangerous road with blind curves, unprotected bends and some very sharp turns.

But this man was not bothered by danger. He knew the road like the back of his hand, and drove carefully. The traffic was always minimal.

One fine Saturday morning as he was approaching a curve, suddenly, from around the corner came a car, swerving dangerously and almost out of control! He just managed to avoid a direct impact before it steadied back onto its own side of the road. Passing him, the flustered woman driver stuck her head out of the window and yelled, 'Pig!'

Greatly offended, the man mustered what he felt was an appropriate response and shouted back, 'Cow!' before the driver disappeared.

'It was her fault, she was in my lane,' he was grumbling to himself as he rounded the next bend and ran straight into a pig!

Criticism reflects the critic

- Rembrandt is not to be compared in the painting of character with our extraordinary gifted English artist , Mr Rippingille. (John Hunt 1775–1848)
- 'Far too noisy, my dear Mozart. Far too many notes,' said the Emperor Ferdinand after the first performance of *The Marriage of Figaro*!
- 'Flight by machines heavier than air is unpractical and insignificant, if not utterly impossible,' wrote Simon Newcombe (1835–1919) whose opinion was not changed by the success of the Wright brothers just 18 months later
- 'You will never amount to very much,' said a Munich schoolmaster to the ten-year-old Albert Einstein
- 'They could not hit an elephant at this dist …' These were the last words of General John Sedgwick as he peered out over enemy lines during the Battle of Spotsylvania in 1864.
- 'We don't like their sound. Groups of guitars are on their way out,' was the judgement of Decca Recording Company as they turned down The Beatles in 1962.[8]

Sometimes the critics are right

We should always try to evaluate what the critic has said. Even a wrong motive for making the criticism may not devalue it. Once the immediate emotion is calmed the mind can carefully weigh it up. The questions must arise.

Is there some way I need to change?

Would I be willing to change under any circumstance? If not, why not?

What positive steps can I possibly take to respond as a damage limitation?

'Faithful are the wounds of a friend' (Proverbs 27:6 KJV).

What should I do?
'He who listens to a life-giving rebuke will be at home among the wise.' (Proverbs 15:31 NIV)

Once, when King Hezekiah received an unwelcome letter he 'spread it out before the Lord.' (2 Kings 19:14) This is the best place to take any problem.

'He was oppressed ... yet he opened not his mouth ... as a sheep before her shearers is dumb, so he openeth not his mouth.' (Isaiah 53:7 KJV)

Classic response
President Abraham Lincoln once said:

> If I tried to answer all the attacks made on me, this shop might as well be closed for any other business. I do the best I know how and I mean to keep doing so. If the end brings me out right, then what is said won't matter. If the end brings me out wrong, then ten angels declaring I was right would make no difference.

Good advice
Never fear criticism when you are right; never ignore criticism when you are wrong. (Anon) There may be something you need to do about rectifying something that's wrong.

I remember once discussing criticism with the late John Wimber and he just shook his head sympathetically. 'I try to do what Paul did shipwrecked on the island of Malta when a viper came out of the firewood and bit him. He just shook it off!'

You'll never please all
An old man and his son were taking their donkey to market. As they passed some people along the way they overheard a comment:

'Look at that silly pair – walking when they could be riding comfortably.'

It seemed a sensible idea to the old man, so he and the boy mounted the donkey and continued along the way. Soon they passed another group.

'Look at that lazy pair,' said a voice, 'breaking the back of that poor donkey, tiring him out so that no one will want to buy him.'

So the old man dismounted leaving the boy to ride while he walked alongside. Soon they heard yet more criticism:

'What a terrible thing, that old man walking while his young boy rides the donkey!'

So they changed places but soon they heard yet more whisperings:

'What a terrible thing – that big strong man riding while making the little boy walk.'

The old man and the boy considered the situation and in the end decided to continue their journey carrying the donkey slung between them on a pole. As they crossed the bridge leading into town, the donkey broke loose, fell into the river and drowned. The moral of this tale is that you will never please everyone. (*Aesop's Fables*)

THOUGHTS

Sometimes we are so busy adding up our troubles that we forget to count our blessings. We forget that God is a specialist; he is well able to work our failures into his plans. If money is a basis for judging success or failure; it is obvious that Jesus Christ was a failure![9] (Erwin Lutzer)

POEM

(Found tucked into an old Bible)
Be strong, be strong,
We are not here to dream,
To drift,
There are battles to fight,
And loads to lift;
Shun not the battle,
'Tis God's gift,
Be strong, be strong.
It matters not how
Deep entrenched the wrong,
Faint not, fight on,
Tomorrow comes the song
Be strong, be strong.

PRAYERS

Lord, You said I am blessed when they revile and persecute me, and say all kinds of evil against me falsely for your sake (Matthew 5:11,12), but it's so hard Lord! When you were reviled you reviled not again. And as a lamb before his shearers was silent so you opened not your mouth (Isaiah 53:7b).

It hurt me Lord,
I felt something torn,
Something unbalanced,
Like a mechanism gone wrong,
Like a man with broken bones.
And I reflected that what you had planned was good,
And that there can be no order and beauty, love and joy outside your plan.

(Extract from a reflective prayer by Michel Quoist)

They are saying things that are not true;
O blessed Lord, what shall I do?
He answers, 'What is that to thee?
Thy duty is to follow Me.' (Anon)

Lord, help me to handl these things as you triumphantly endured them when you lived among us. O God, grant me the grace of such patience and tolerance for the sake of your kingdom and glory. Amen.

CHAPTER 20

People who handle success maturely

Everyone was saying that I was doing really well,
but something inside me was telling me that my success
was putting my own soul in danger.

(HENRI NOUWEN)

Try not to become a person of success,
but rather try to become a person of value.

(ALBERT EINSTEIN)

The word 'success' has cropped up many times in this book. It's hard to avoid it even though one dislikes using such terms when talking of Christian leadership, because the word conveys an implication of unchristian vices. The Preacher wrote, 'I observed that the basic motive for success is the driving force of envy and jealousy!' (Ecclesiastes 4:4 Living Bible). Jesus, in his sermon on the mount, says 'How sad when everybody says, "You're wonderful". Your fathers said the same about lying prophets.'

ASPIRATION OF IMMATURITY
In discussing the meaning of life John Hambre, a member of a Washington Think Tank said:

Here, [in America] the desire for money and success is the measure. At some point we have to move from success to significance. If we don't manage that, life will be soulless and unfulfilling and that is corrosive to a society. We have a lot of growing up to do. We are still at the adolescent stage.

Peter Mandelson, a cabinet member under Tony Blair's premiership from which he had to resign twice, blamed the destruction of his political career on his addiction to publicity. (in a 'Tabloid Tales' broadcast on 8 May 2003) In retrospect he believed he was seduced by his own media image: 'I started to enjoy the publicity,' he admitted in a TV interview. 'I committed the mortal sin with good publicity or external publicity: instead of just enjoying it, I inhaled it and I think I probably inhaled a bit too much.'

Success can be an addictive and destructive thing.

Pride is very subtle. When we try to be humble it is so easy to feel proud of even that. It was cleverly, but snidely, said of T. E. Lawrence (*The Seven Pillars of Wisdom*) that 'he was forever backing into the limelight'!

SUCCESS SO EASILY LEADS TO FAILURE

Speaking at a recent conference in England, Dallas Willard talked of the same problem when he asked: 'How many people fall apart when they succeed?' His inference obviously was that he knew of too many leaders who did just that. But his question raises two further questions

1. What do we really understand by success?

Are we talking about numerical growth in the congregation? A new church building or an extension we have put up? The income of the church or the amount of money we earn? Or our position in the church's hierarchy?

These are hardly marks of success in the light of Christ's own ministry. He was undoubtedly the most successful leader ever, yet he built no large church and when he died he had relatively few possessions or disciples. Success for a Christian leader can never be evaluated in such ways.

2. Who would ever dare to consider him/herself a success?

'You also, when you have done everything you were told to do, should say "We are unworthy servants; we have only done our duty"' says the Lord. (Luke 17:10 NIV)

'What cries I uttered up to you, my God, when I read the Psalms of David, songs of faith ... which exclude the boastful mind.' (St. Augustine, *Confessions*)

The hardest secret for a man to keep is his opinion of himself and there is nothing so off-putting as a big head. 'None are so empty as those who are full of themselves.' (Benjamin Whichcote)

MISCONCEPTION OF HUMAN DIGNITY

In October 1989 Archbishop Robert Runcie issued a warning to Carol Kennedy, deputy editor of *Director*, about the rise of a new pharisaism:

> The successful are always tempted to regard their success as a sort of blessing or reward for righteousness. This can lead to judgements being made about the unsuccessful, the unemployed, the poor and the unintelligent which are both uncharitable and untrue. Those attitudes reduce human dignity.

It is difficult to disguise self-centredness, but it is far from what God wants in his leaders. Jesus 'who, for the joy set before him endured the Cross', superbly modelled great leadership. He taught his disciples specifically:

> In this world the kings and great men order their people around, and yet they are called 'friends of the people'. But among you, those who are the greatest should take the lowest rank, and the *leader* should be like a *servant*. Normally the master sits at the table and is served by his servants. But not here! For I am your servant (Luke 22:25–27 NLT, emphasis mine).

FAITHFULNESS AND FRUITFULNESS

What other word can we substitute for success? The word smacks of achieving in a career, and Christian leaders should rather think of their high calling. 'Career' suggests upward mobility whereas a 'calling' may involve a moving downward into humble acts of service and 'taking the lowest seat'. A career is something I choose for myself. My calling is something God has chosen for me. A career implies advancement, status, money, power, and even popularity, whereas a vocation involves sacrifice, suffering, poverty, being 'despised and rejected of men' and even being counted, like St Paul, as one of 'the offscourings' of the earth.

But if the opposite of success is considered failure, sadly an accurate description of the process of decline in the Western church today, then surely we could do with a few more 'successful' churches to increase membership etc. If success means effectiveness that is an obvious blessing, but if it is considered a stepping stone to self-aggrandisement it is a serious mistake. Much better would be the use of the biblical words 'faithfulness' and 'fruitfulness'. That is what God is looking for. 'It is required of a steward that he be found faithful.' And it is true faithfulness that produces real fruitfulness.

Fruitfulness manifests itself in a myriad ways, even in just a loving deed, a single convert or a saintly life. Good leaders learn to see secret prayer and fasting, failures, vulnerability and humility, as the unseen paths to fruitfulness in the eyes of God. This is the way to handle success effectively

QUOTES
- Success can dispose us to dangerous consequences. (Anon)
- It's a tragedy when a young man succeeds before his time. (Martyn Lloyd-Jones)
- Success tends to breed arrogance, complacency and isolation. (Max DePree)
- Success can close the mind faster than prejudice. (Anon)
- Success: the one unpardonable sin against one's fellow man. (Ambrose Bierce)
- Success is fragile like a butterfly. We usually crush the life out of it in our efforts to possess it. (Max DePree)
- The key to succeeding in the system lies in the way we exploit our freedom, make our choices, and anticipate the consequences. (Anon)
- If you build a big business you're a sinister influence; if you don't you're a failure. (Anon)
- Behind every successful man there is a good woman telling him he does not amount to much. (Anon)
- When success turns a man's head, he faces failure. (Anon)
- Success is getting what you want; happiness is wanting what you get. (Anon)
- Success [in leadership] is defined as the progressive realisation of a predetermined goal. (John C. Maxwell)
- Every leader's past success and failure can be a source of

wisdom for the future. (Anon)
- Success is moving from one failure to another with enthusiasm. (Winston Churchill)
- Success is not for ever, and failure isn't fatal. (Don Shula)
- He was a legend in his own lunch hour! (Anon)
- I can handle fame because I've seen it coming all along(!) (Daly Thompson)
- When you are as great as I am, it's hard to be humble. (Mohammed Ali)
- Dim your lights so that others can see. (Ruth Yule)
- I hate the big time, I feel the loss of friends terribly. I have to have bouncers at my birthday parties now. (James Hunt, champion racing driver)
- One thing I do suffer from is overconfidence. It's something I'm working on. (George Foreman, Heavy-weight boxing champion)
- Nobody ever beats Wales at Rugby, they just score more points. (Graham Mourie, New Zealand captain)
- Ability will enable a man to go to the top, but it takes character to keep him there. (Anon)
- Every hero becomes a bore at last. (Ralph Waldo Emerson)
- We try to climb to a high position when God has ordained that we go down. (A. W. Tozer)
- The way to up is down. (Donald Barnhouse)
- I have tried to move up and up, and you have tried to move down and down. (Herbert Morrison to Lord Longford)
- Better the loss that makes them humble than the success that makes them proud. (Thomas Watson)
- I'm so sick of Holy Ghost superstars. (Black Bishop Kenneth Ulmer)

ILLUSTRATIONS
Death by adulation

I read a newspaper story a while back about an actress who was killed by her own press cuttings. She was reaching up for something in her wardrobe when the big box in which she stored them fell on her head [and killed her]. (Simon Parke, *Church Times*, 5 March 2004).

Servant leadership

A headmaster was noted for the way that he walked around carrying a tray on important parents' days, serving simple cups of tea, when he could have been out strutting about among the grateful parents receiving accolades.

Leading by example

The reason Ernest Shackleton, the Antarctic explorer, is still such compelling reading today isn't just that he survived against incredible odds, but he succeeded in the important things.

> 'We long for the teamwork and camaraderie that the Boss [Shackleton] inspired,' one of his party wrote. 'We admire his ability to recognise both the faults and potential of his men, and his willingness to lead by example. We empathise with the loneliness that haunted his tough decisions. And we praise his understanding that respect for human life trumps any short-term prize. Ultimately, Shackleton is a success because, in him we catch glimpses of who we want to be.' (Jonathan Karpoff, Finance Professor, University of Washington)

A warning

Henry Ford, who pioneered the Ford Eight, popularly known as the people's car and painted black, was a radical thinker as a young man making his name. But after years of success, when the sales of Ford Eights began to decline, and other car manufacturers were selling better, his juniors begged him to be able to offer the same Ford Eight in a variety of colours.

He will long be remembered for his classic reply which marred his reputation: 'You can have any colour you like so long as it is black.' One can too easily get stuck in the old ways of thinking instead of letting the mind be renewed.

It's wise to go for the small things first

Rudolph Giuliani, who achieved major transformations during his eight years as Mayor of New York City, soon built up a reputation with a deliberately selected series of small, but significant, achievements.

Jesus articulated this principle quite simply: 'He who is faithful in what is least is faithful also in much' (Luke 16:10 NKJV). Early achievements in lesser things will build up the supporters' confidence for the bigger triumphs later.

Rudolph Giuliani continues, 'These early successes, while not of major significance on their own, provided critical evidence that plans could be put into action'. Use success humbly and wisely as a platform for pressing on to tougher objectives.

BIBLE QUOTE

'For I say, through the grace given unto me, to every man that is among you, not to think of himself more highly than he ought to think; but to think soberly, according as God hath dealt to every man the measure of faith' (Romans 12:3 KJV).

A POEM

Is your place a small place?
Tend it with care! – He set you there.
Is your place a large place?
Guard it with care! – He set you there.
What e'er your place, it is
Not yours alone, but His
Who set you there!

(John Oxenham)

PRAYERS

Oh God, forgive me for my stupidity, my blindness in success, my lack of trust in Thee. Be Thou now my Saviour in success. Save me from conceit. Save me from pettiness. Save me from myself. And take this success, I pray, and use it for Thy glory. In Thy strength, I pray. Amen. (Peter Marshall)

Teach us, good Lord,
To serve you as you deserve:
To give, and not to count the cost;
To fight and not to heed the wounds;
To toil, and not to seek for rest;
To labour, and not to ask for any reward,
Except that of knowing that we do thy holy will

(San Ignacio Loyola)

Lord I do not pray for tasks equal to my strength: but for strength equal to my tasks. (Bishop Phillips Brooks)

POSTCRIPT

If we are still asking the question 'Can anyone be a leader?' the answer must obviously be 'No'. But we must very quickly follow this up by saying that anyone is a potential leader who is seriously committed to cultivating the qualities outlined in this book.

You will be a blessing to all those who follow your lead as a labourer in the kingdom of God.

BIBLIOGRAPHY

Adair, J, *Effective Leadership*, Pan Books, 1983.

Allen, Roland, *Missionary Methods: St Paul's or Ours*, World Dominion Press, 1956.

Ashton, Cyrel, *Servant Spirit-Serving Churches*, Marshall Pickering, 1988.

Baker, Joel Arthur, *Paradigms: Business of discovering the future*, HarperCollins Publishers, April 1993.

Baker, Philip, *Wisdom – the Forgotten Factor of Success*, MacPherson's Printing Group, 1998.

Batchelor, Mary (Ed), *The Lion Prayer Collection*, Lion Publishing, 1996.

Barna, George, *Leaders on Leadership*, Regal, 1997.

Barna, George, *The Power of Vision*, Regal, 1992.

Bell, Alan (ed.), *The Sayings of Sydney Smith*, Duckworth, 1993.

Birkinshaw, J. & Crainer, S, *Leadership the Sven-Goran Eriksson Way*, Capstone, 2002.

Blanchard, K. & Shula, D, *The Little Book of Coaching*, Harper Collins, 2001.

Brearley, Mike, *The Art of Captaincy*, Hodder & Stoughton, 1983.

Callahan, Kennon L., *Twelve Keys to an Effective Leadership*, Harper & Row, 1987.

Carey, George, *The Church in the Market Place*, Kingsway, 1984.

Cassidi, Deborah, (Compiler), *Favourite Prayers*, Cassell, 1999.

Castle, T. A., *Treasury of Christian Wisdom*, Hodder & Stoughton, 2001.

Cocksworth, C, & Brown, R., *Being a Priest Today*, Canterbury Press, 2002.

Cocksworth, Christopher, *Holy, Holy, Holy*, Darton, Longman & Todd, 1997.

Cocksworth, Christopher, *Wisdom: the Spirit's Gift*, Grove Books Limited.

Coleman, Daniel, *The New Leaders*, Little Brown, 2002.

Coleman, Daniel, *Emotional Intelligence*, Bantam Books, 1995.

Colquhoun, Frank, *New Parish Prayers*, Hodder & Stoughton, 1982.

Colson, Charles, *The Body – Being Light in Darkness*, Word Publishing, 1992.

Cotter John P. and Lawrence, Paul R., *Mayors in Action*, John Wiley and Sons, 1974.

Crompton, Richmal, *William and the School Report*, Macmillan Children's Books.

Cymbala, Jim, *Fresh Wind, Fresh Fire*, Zondervan, 1997.

De Bono, Edward, *How To Be More Interesting*, Penguin Books, 1997.

De Bono, Edward, *Lateral Thinking*, Penguin Books, 1970.

DePree, Max, *Leadership Jazz*, Dell Publishing, 1992.

DePree, Max, *Leadership is an Art*, Dell Publishing, 1989.

DePree, Max, *Leading Without Power*, Jossey Bass, 1997.

The Devil's Dictionary, 1906

Dortch, Richard, *Integrity: How I Lost It and My Journey Back*, Green Forest, New Leaf Press, 1991.

Drucker, Peter, in *The Leader of the Future*, Eds. Hesselbein, Goldsmith and Beckhard, Jossey Bass.

Edwards, David L, *Religion and Change*, Hodder & Stoughton, 1969.
Edwards, David L, *The Church That Could Be*, SPCK, 2002.
Eims, Leroy, *Be the Leader You were Meant to Be*, Victor Books, 1983.
Fitzel, Hans, *Top Ten Mistakes Leaders Make*, Vistor Books, 2004.
Ford, Kevin, *Jesus for a New Generation*, IVP, 1995.
Foster, Jack, *Ideaship*, Berret Koehler Publishing, 2001.
Freeman, J. Stephen (ed), *Shaping our Future*, Cowley Publications, 1994.
Fry, John W., *Jesus the Pastor*, Zondervan, 2000.
Gamble, Robin, *The Irrelevant Church*, Monarch, 1991.
Gary and Prahalad,C.K., *Competing for the Future*, Boston, Harvard Business School
    Press, 1944.
George, Carl E., *Prepare Your Church for the Future*, Fleming H. Revell, 1884.
Gough, Basil, *The Man Behind The Ministry*, Falcon Books, 1964.
Grant, Gary, *Sacred Pathways*, Ad Donker Publishers, 2002.
Green, Michael, *Freed to Serve*, Hodder & Stoughton, 1983.
Green, Michael, *But Don't All Religions Lead to God?* IVP, 2002.
Green, Michael, *Adventure of Faith*, Harper Collins, 2001.
Greenslade, S. L., *Shepherding the Flock*, SCM Press, 1967
Guiliani, R. *Leadership*, Little Brown, 2002.
Gunstone, John, *A People for His Praise*, Hodder & Stoughton, 1978.
Handy, Charles, *Understanding Organizations*, Penguin, 1976.
Harper, Michael, *Let My People Grow*, Hodder & Stoughton, 1977.
Harvard Business Review on Breakthrough Leadership, Harvard Business School Press,
    2001.
Haward, Steven F., *Churchill On Leadership*, Forum, 1998.
Hesse lben, Frances, et al, *The Leader of the Future*, Drucker Foundation Series Press,
    1906)
Hood, George, *Neither a Bang nor a Wimper*, Singapore, 1991.
Hughes, Bryan, *Leadership Tool-Kit*, Monarch, 1988.
Hughes, Gerard W., *Oh God Why?* BRF, 1993.
Hughes, John, *The Pastor's Notebook*, Kingsway, 2003.
Hybels, Bill, et al: *Leadership by the Book*, Harper Collins, 2001.
Hybels, Bill, *Courageous Leadership*, Zondervan, 2002.
Jamieson, Alan, *A Churchless Faith*, SPCK, 2002.
Johnson, Dwight L., *The Transparent Leader*, Harvest House, 2001.
Kennedy, Carol, *Guide to Management Gurus*, Random House, 1991.
Kennedy, John F., *Profiles in Courage*, Harper Collins, 2000.
Kew, R. & White, R.J., *New Millennium + New Church*, Cowley Publications, 1992.
King, Philip, *Leadership Explosion*, Hodder & Stoughton, 1987.
Kouzes J.M. & Posner, Barry Z., *The Leadership Challenge*, Jossey Bass, 1995.
Lewis, Phillip, V., *Transformational Leadership*, Broadman & Holman, 1996.
Lord, Walter, in *The Good Years*, Black Dog & Leventhal Publishers, 1960.
Lutzer, Erwin, *Failure – the Backdoor to Success*, Moody Press, 1999.
Marshall, Tom, *Understanding Leadership*, Sovereign World, 1991.
Maughan, W. Somerset, *Of Human Bondage*, Indypublish.com 2002.
Maxwell, John C., *Failing Forward*, Thomas Nelson, 2000.
Maxwell, John C., *Developing the Leader Within You*, Thomas Nelson, 1993.

Maxwell, John C., *Developing the Leaders Around You*, Thomas Nelson, 1995.

Maxwell, John C., *Minutes in a Leader's Day*, Thomas Nelson, 2000.

Maxwell, John C., *Laws of Leadership*, Thomas Nelson, 1998.

Maxwell, John C., *The Power of Leadership*, Eagle, 2002.

Maxwell, John C., *Your Attitude: Key to Success*, Thomas Nelson, 1984.

McIntosh, Gary, 'Worship and Church Growth', *Journal of the American Society of Church Growth 7*, 1996.

Michael, Larry J., *Spurgeon on Leadership*, Kregel Publications, 2003.

Morrell, M & Capperell, S, *Shackleton's Way*, Nicholas Brearly Publishing, 2001.

Moynagh, Michael, *Changing World, Changing Church*, Monarch Books, 2001.

Nazir-Ali, Michael, *Shapes of the Church To Come*, Kingsway, 2001.

Noll, Mark A., *The Scandal of the Evangelical Mind*, IVP, 1994.

Pacetta, Frank, *Don't Fire Them – Fire Them Up*, Simon & Schuster, 1994.

Paine, Gustavus S., *The Men Behind the KJV*, Baker Book House, 1988.

Paterson, Robert, *Christian Wisdom*, Monarch Books, 1997.

Peale, Norman Vincent, *The Power of Positive Thinking*, Vermillion, 2000.

Peters, Tom, and Waterman, Robert, *In Search Of Excellence*, HarperCollins Publishers, 1982.

Phillips, Donald, T., *Lincoln on Leadership*, Little, Brown and Co, 1992.

Phillips-Jones, Linda, *Mentors and Protégés*, Coalition of Counseling Centers, 2001.

Pile, Stephen, *The Book of Heroic Failures*, Penguin Books, 1989.

Piper, John, *A Godward Life*, Multnomah Publishers, 1997.

Pollock, J.C., *Shaftesbury: The Poor Man's Earl*, Hodder & Stoughton, 1986.

Pulkingham, Graham, *They Left Their Nets*, Hodder, 1974.

Pytches, David, *Leadership For New Life*, Hodder & Stoughton, 1998.

Quoist, Michel, *Prayers of Life*, Gill & Macmillan, 1963.

Roy, J., *The Battle of Dienbienphu*, Harper & Row, 1965.

Rush, Myron, *Management: A Biblical Approach*, Victor Books, 1987.

Ryle, J. C., *Holiness*, Hodder & Stoughton, 1996.

Ryle, James, *A Dream Come True*, Eagle Publishing, 1995.

Schwarz, Christian A., *Natural Church Development*, ChurchSmart Resources, 1996.

Scotland, Nigel, *Living with a Purpose*, Scripture Union, 1988.

Shearman, David, *The Unstoppable Church*, Sovereign World.

Sheppard, David, *Built as a City*, Hodder & Stoughton, 1974.

Snyder Howard A., *New Wineskins*, Marshall, Morgan & Scott. 1977.

Steven, James H.S., *Worship in the Spirit*, Paternoster Press, 2002.

Spurgeon, C.H., *Lectures to My Younger Students*, Zondervan Publishing House, 1955.

Storms, Sam, *Pleasures for Evermore*, NavPress Publishing Group, 2000.

Stott, John, *Obeying Christ in a Changing World*, Collins, 1977.

Taylor, David, *The Naked Leader*, Bantam Books, 2003.

Thompson, Kevin M., *The Company Culture Book*, Prentice Hall, 2002.

Tiller J. and Birchall M., *The Gospel Community*, Marshall, Morgan & Scott, 1987.

Tofler, Alvin, *Future Shock*, Pan Books, 1970.

Tournier, Paul, *The Adventure of Living*, Highland Books.

Townsend, Robert, *Up the Organisation*, Michael Joseph, 1970.

Wagner, Peter, *Spiritual Power and Church Growth*, Strang Communications, 1986.

Wagner, Peter, *The New Apostolic Churches*, Regal,1998.

Ward, Pete, *Liquid Church*, Hendrickson Publishers, 2002.

Warren, Robert, *On the Anvil*, Highland Books, 1990.

Warren, Robert, *Being Human, Being Church*, Marshall Pickering, 1995.

White, John, *Excellence in Leadership*, IVP, 1986.

Williamson, Mabel, *Have we NO RIGHT?* Lutterworth Press, 1958.

Wurmbrand, Richard, *Alone With God*, Hodder & Stoughton, 1988.

Yun, Brother and Hattaway, Paul, *The Heavenly Man*, Monarch Books, 2002.

ENDNOTES

Introduction

1. J. Tiller J. and M. Birchall, M. *The Gospel Community*, Marshall, Morgan & Scott, 1987, p 64.
2. Christian A. Schwarz, *Natural Church Development*, Church Smart Resources, 1996.
3. David Sheppard, Built as a City, Hodder & Stoughton, 1974, pp 255-6.
4. Most managements complain about the lack of able people and go outside to fill key positions. Nonsense! Nobody inside an organisation ever looked ready to move into a bigger job. I use the rule of 50 per cent. Try to find somebody inside the company with a record of success (in any area) and with an appetite for the job. If he looks like 50 per cent of what you need, give him the job. In six months he'll have grown the other 50 per cent and everybody will be satisfied.

    How to do it wrong: go outside and get some expensive guy who looks like 100 per cent of what you want and a year later, after having raised salaries all around him, you'll still be teaching him the business. The people around him will be frustrated and ineffective.

    One of the keys is to pick someone within the company who has a well-deserved reputation as a winner. Not someone who looks to you like a potential winner but doesn't happen to be fitting in very well where he is. The organization will rally around an accepted winner, even when he's temporarily over his head, because in their eyes he deserves the chance. The phony who conned you into giving him the job will go down for the third time and pull down everybody else he can reach. Robert Townsend, 'Promotions from Within' by Robert Townsend in *Up The Organisation*, Michael Joseph, London, p 145.
5. Philip King, *Leadership Explosion*, Hodder & Stoughton, 1987, p 162.
6. Researchers have demonstrated that in the Agricultural 'Revolt of the Field' in 1874 the representation of Methodism was as follows. In Suffolk seventy-nine men, out of a total of 170 union leaders, who were active speakers, chairmen, or officials were identifiable as Methodists. In Norfolk 273 out of a total of the 525 union leaders were Methodists. In Lincolnshire 134 out 254 were identified as Methodists. (Cf Nigel Scotland, *Methodism and the Revolt of the Field*, Alan Sutton, p58.

Chapter 1

1. Charles Handy, *Understanding Organizations*, Penguin, 1999.
2. John Richardson, *New Directions*, October 2003.
3. Bill Hybels, *Courageous Leadership*, Zondervan, 2002, p 26.
4. Jonty Driver, *Daily Telegraph*, 29th January 2003.
5. In Acts 20:17, the leaders are referred to as 'elders' (*presbuteros*), and called to

shepherd or 'pastor the flock' (*poimnio*) over which they have been set by the Holy Spirit as 'overseers' (or bishops/*episkopous*) (v 28). These terms all describe the same group of leaders.

The pastors (leaders) in the New Testament are sometimes referred to as elders, and sometimes as overseers or bishops. The ministries under their oversight are many and varied and the lack of a fully defined structure for a New Testament church allows them to be reconfigured with maximum flexibility. As the New Testament churches grew, the pastoral leadership soon appeared to have been officially shared in a supportive role by deacons (*diakonia*) with special responsibilities in the local church. This is not to overlook the fact that the whole church is intended to be a universal diaconate – all God's people are *diakonia* – called to serve with their individual giftings (1 Corinthians 12:7–11), just as all believers are priests (1 Peter 2:5).

Many local churches soon became organised themselves to help the leading pastor in the exercise of his/her local ministry, while the apostles, prophets, evangelists and teachers (Ephesians 4:11) developed the church universally with their more specialised ministries: guarding the faith and church planting (apostles); proclaiming God's Word (prophets); finding other sheep which, Jesus said 'are not of this fold' (John 10:16) (evangelists); teaching in and across the local churches (teachers). Those taking over the pastoral care of the new church plants were called shepherds (pastors). The pastor was also the key person to help the local church members and kept them aware of the suffering, oppressed and needy world outside the congregation. And the leaders of the local churches led their people to pray and financially resourced the apostles, prophets, evangelists, pastors and teachers.

6. Mike Brearley,. *The Art of Captaincy*, Hodder & Stoughton, 1983.

7. J. Birkinshaw J. & S. Crainer, S. *Leadership the Sven Goran Eriksson Way*, Capstone, 2002, p.124.

8. Spoken by the blind Colonel Frank Slade to the boy Charles Simms in the film, *The Scent of a Woman*.

9. Robert Goizueta led Coca Cola from a company worth $4 billion to one worth $150 billion, an increase of more than 3,500%; the second most important corporation in N. America in its time.

10. Parody of Caesar's Latin quote

11. John Hiscock writes of his interview with Kevin Spacey as he contemplates taking up his new post as artistic director at the Old Vic.

12. M. Morrell and S. Capparell, *Shackleton's Way*, Nicholas Brealy Publishing, 2001.

13. One-time president of Carrier Corporation's European air conditioning business and General Manager of Westinghouse Electric's synthetic fuels business.

14. Robert Sutton in *Sunday Telegraph*, Business File, 26 May 2002.

15. Morrell & Capparell, op. cit.

Chapter 2

1. Gerard W. Hughes, *Oh God Why?* BRF, 1993.

2. John Gunstone, *A People for His Praise*, Hodder & Stoughton, 1978, p 90.

3. Ibid. p 103.
4. Nigel Scotland, *Living with a Purpose*, Scripture Union, 1988.
5. Gary Grant *Sacred Pathways,* Ad Donker Publishers, 2002.
6. Bill Hybels, *Courageous Leadership*, Zondervan, 2002, p 218.
7. Gunstone, op.cit. pp 101–2.
8. George Carey, *The Church in the Market Place*, Kingsway, 1984.
9. John Piper, *A Godward Life*, Multnomah Publishers, 1997.

Chapter 3
1. A final part of Martin Luther King's last speech before his assassination in Memphis.
2. George Carey, *The Church in the Market Place*, Kingsway, 1984, p. 85.
3. Pete Ward, *Liquid Church*, Hendrickson Publishers, 2002.
4. Richard Wurmbrand, *Alone with God*, Hodder & Stoughton, 1988, p 90.
5. Brother Yun, *The Heavenly Man*, Monarch Books, 2002.
6. Robert Townsend, *Up the Organisation*, Michael Joseph, 1970, p 53.
7. Article commenting on recent defeat of the Democrats in US, *Church Times*, 15 November 2002.
8. Graham Pulkingham, *They Left Their Nets*, Hodder, 1974.
9. Bill Hybels, *Courageous Leadership*, Zondervan, 2002.
10. Joel Arthur Baker, *Paradigms: Business of Discovering the Future*, HarperCollins Publishers, 1993.

Chapter 4
1. Cambridge University Library.
2. J. C. Ryle, *Holiness*, Hodder & Stoughton, 1996.

Chapter 5
1. Mark A. Noll, *The Scandal of the Evangelical Mind*, IVP, 1994, p.26.
2. Robert Warren, *On the Anvil*, Highland Books, 1990, p 176-7.
3. William Hague, writing of George Bush in the *Sunday Telegraph*, 6 October 2002.

Chapter 6
1. Christopher Cocksworth, *Wisdom, the Spirit's Gift*, Grove Books.
2. Alexandr Solzhenitsyn, *Warning to the Western World*, Panorama, BBC, March 1976.
3. Cocksworth, op. cit.
4. Walter Lord, *The Good Years*, HarperCollins Publishers, 1960.

Chapter 7
1. C. S. Lewis, *The Screwtape Letters*, HarperCollins.
2. Mabel Williamson, *Have we NO RIGHT?* Lutterworth Press, 1958.
3. James Ryle, *A Dream Come True*, Eagle Publishing, 1995.

4. Charles H. Spurgeon, *Lectures to my Younger Students*, Zondervan, 1955.
5. Bill Hybels et al., *Leadership by the Book*, HarperCollins, 1999, p 196.
6. Peter Drucker, in *The Leader of the Future*, Eds. Hesselbein, Goldsmith and Beckhard, Jossey Bass.
7. Ron Draper, *How Sven Plotted a Quiet Revolution*, www.soccernet.com

Chapter 8
1. Caption over a review of Fred Archer's life in the *Daily Telegraph*, 27.12. 2003.
2. Frank Pacetta, *Don't Fire Them – Fire Them Up*, Simon & Schuster, 1994.
3. Both are quotes from *Breakthrough Leadership*, Harvard Business Review Paperback Series, p 43.
4. John Hiscock writes of his interview with Kevin Spacey as he faces his new post as artistic director at the Old Vic.
5. Daniel Goleman, *Emotional Intelligence*, Bantam Books, 1995.
6. Ken Blanchard and Don Shula, *The Little Book of Coaching*, HarperCollins, 2001.
7. *Il Messeggero*, Rome's popular daily newspaper reporting on the publication of Mother Teresa's diaries.

Chapter 9
1. Bill Hybels, *Courageous Leadership*, Zondervan, 2002, p 185.
2. Richard Dortch, *Integrity: How I Lost It and My Journey Back*, Green Forest, New Leaf Press, 1991, p 128.
3. Ken Blanchard and Don Shula, *The Little Book of Coaching*, HarperCollins, 2001.
4. W. Somerset Maughan, *Of Human Bondage*, Indypublish.com 2002.
5. Charles Colson, *The Body: Being Light in Darkness*, Word Publishing, 1992.

Chapter 11
1. Canon David Winter, later Head of BBC Religious Broadcasting, remembering one of his predecessors, *Church Times*, 3 January 2003.

Chapter 12
1. Paul Super writing of the great missionary statesman Dr. John R. Mott.
2. Ibid.

Chapter 13
1. Robert Warren, *On the Anvil*, Highland Books, 1990, p.36.
2. Philip Baker, *Wisdom*, Authentic Lifestyle, 1992.
3. J.C. Pollock, *Shaftesbury: The Poor Man's Earl*, Hodder & Stoughton, 1986.
4. The physicist aboard the *Discovery* writing of Sir Ernest Shackleton, the explorer.

Chapter 14
1. An aspect of Dr Cross's selection process for admission to the University of London Medical School.
2. Comment from the Captain of the *Endurance* about Sir Ernest Shackleton.

Chapter 15
1. David Taylor, *The Naked Leader*, Bantam Books, 2003.
2. Lincoln's reason for relieving General John C. Freemost from his command in Missouri during America's Civil War, 9 September 1861.
3. Culled from *Leadership in a Combat Zone*.
4. *In Search Of Excellence* by Tom Peters and Robert Waterman, HarperCollins, 1982.
5. Donald T. Phillips, *Lincoln on Leadership*, Little, Brown, 1992.
6. Diary entry by Orde-Lees, one of Ernest Shackleton's crew members.
7. J. Roy, *The Battle of Dienbienphu*, Harper & Row, 1965, p 304, cited in Philip King's *Leadership Explosion*.

Chapter 16
1. Myron Rush, *Management: Biblical Approach*, Victor Books, 1987.

Chapter 17
1. See Gary McIntosh, 'Worship and Church Growth', *Journal of the American Society of Church Growth 7*, 1996, p 1.
2. History of Christian Education.

Chapter 19
1. J. M. Kouzes & Barry Z. Posner, *The Leadership Challenge*, Jossey Bass, 1995, p68.
2 *Sir Earnest Shackleton: The Intrepid Explorer.*
3. Richmal Crompton, *William and the School Report*, Macmillan Children's Books.
4. Bill Hybels, *Courageous Leadership*, Zondervan, 2002, p 178.
5. Robert Warren, *On the Anvil*, Highland Books, 1990, p 39.
6. Republican Senator G.W. Norris of Nebraska by John F. Kennedy quoted in his *Profiles in Courage*, HarperCollins, 2000.
7. Nominated Sportsman of the Year in 1993 by America's *Sports Illustrated* for becoming the winning coach in National Football League history.
8. With apologies for six adaptations from *The Book of Heroic Failures* by Stephen Pile.
9. Erwin Lutzer, *Failure – the Backdoor to Success*, Moody Press, 1999.

EPILOGUE

WATCHING THE TORCH PASS

Power with men - it has much appeal.
Can't measure its length 'cause it's mostly the feel;
It's the honour, it's the praise, the not being left out,
It's others looking to you as the one with the clout;
It's so easy to swell and to hallow the pride,
So hard to claim meekness and remain humble inside;
Accolades keep coming and you're running to win,
It all seems so right - so distant from sin;
But the glory fades fast with its hue and its cry,
You're just George or you're Mary, whose life has passed by;
The memories remain there, but who wants to listen?
And those really knowing are mostly now missing;
Time passes swiftly! It roars down the pike,
Age swirls around you like floods through the dyke;
Values change quickly in such pressings of time;
It's not really prestige or what ladder you climb,
It's the honour of God whom you soon will face;
It's the gold through the fire that produces true riches;
It's the eye-salve to scratch where each hurting soul itches;
It's white clothing that covers our nakedness and shame;
It's buying from Christ - not the extent of your fame,
That produces rewards that are worthy of praise,
To him be the glory in an eternity of days;
It's the souls God has added through your witness and life,
Multiplying now 'midst Satan's hatred and strife,
Partners forever in the Gospel's Good News!
A body portrait of people in all colours and hues;
'Well done, faithful servant! Now enter your rest,
For you, chosen one, I've reserved what is best!'
                                        (Mark I. Bubeck)

223